The World's Most Powerful Leadership Principle

"A must-read for existing and prospective leaders!"
—Dennis Bakke, CEO emeritus and cofounder,
AES Corporation, "The Global Power Company"

"This book has the power to transform both hearts and minds."
—John Baltes, director,
Silver Dollar City Foundation

"Synovus is committed to developing servant leaders, and this great work will be a helpful tool. It is a true gift to individuals, companies, and our world." —James Blanchard, chairman and CEO,
Synovus Financial Corporation,
#1 on *Fortune*'s "100 Best Companies to Work For"

"This book poignantly reaffirms two fundamental principles that fuel the engines of continuously flourishing businesses: Leadership emanates from character and humility instead of a résumé, and an ounce of action is worth a ton of textbook knowledge."
—Russell Ebeid, president,
Glass Group, Guardian Industries Corporation

"This book takes the concepts presented in *The Servant* and gives the leader the tools needed for 'hardwiring.' This book will leave you better than it found you."
—Brian Jones, director of people development,
Baptist Health Care, #10 on *Fortune*'s
"100 Best Companies to Work For," and recipient
of the 2003 Malcolm Baldrige National Quality Award

"I am a huge fan of Jim's first book, *The Servant;* I give it to all of our managers. I particularly enjoyed the emphasis on application in this work."
— Joy Flora, president,
Merry Maids, a division of ServiceMaster

"I really like this book. Servant leadership is for people of action, and this book is a practical guide to actionable servant leadership."
— Jack Lowe Jr., CEO,
TDIndustries, #2 on *Fortune*'s
"100 Best Companies to Work For," and
Board Chair, Greenleaf Center for Servant-Leadership

"Our company has profited globally from these servant-leadership principles. This book provides the 'road map,' making it easier to realize these benefits at all levels."
— Devin McCarthy, CEO,
Franklynn Industries

"This is a great book and a commonsense approach to leadership. It is time for leaders to realize it is 'morphing time'—time to be the leader their people need and deserve."
— Dale Moore, chairman and CEO,
Moore's Electrical & Mechanical Construction

"This book is the most practical and useful book I have read on servant leadership."
— James Moore Jr., CEO,
Catamount Energy Corporation

"It is refreshing to read a concise book that tells you how to implement ideas rather than just talking theory."
— Kenney Moore, chairman, CEO, and founder,
Andy's Cheesesteaks & Cheeseburgers

"Other leadership books pale in comparison. Our company made Jim Hunter's first book, *The Servant,* required reading. This book is another home run!"
— Dave Skogen, CEO
Festival Foods

"A must-read! This book not only describes what a servant leader looks like but it also provides us with a guide to move ourselves toward becoming that leader."

> — Craig Smith, senior manager of human resources,
> Gordon Food Service

"The principles set forth in this book are timeless. They are part of the eternal laws written into the very nature of mankind."

> — Malcolm R. Sullivan Jr., president,
> Pate-Dawson Company

"This book is a home run! The first read is for a review of servant leadership and to learn the map of implementation. The second and subsequent reads are for a benchmark to one's commitment to change."

> — James Sexton, president and CEO,
> Henry Ford Wyandotte Hospital

"A gift from a servant leader. Clear, comprehensive. It will guide you on your journey toward servant leadership."

> — Robert Thomas, executive director,
> Georgia Servant Leadership Alliance

"Excellent! This book is right on target in offering practical ways to grow servant leaders."

> — Bill Turner, chairman, executive committee,
> Synovus Financial Corporation, #1 on *Fortune*'s
> "100 Best Companies to Work For"

"This practical book provides everything you need to know to begin improving your servant leadership effectiveness, *today*."

> — John Vella, vice president of marketing
> Nestlé Purina PetCare Company

"This book captures the critical element of value creation for any organization: servant leaders at every level. This book teaches us the practical application of the principles of servant leadership."

> — Joe Weller, chairman and CEO,
> Nestlé USA, *Fortune*'s #1 Most Admired Food Company

ALSO BY JAMES C. HUNTER

The Servant

The World's Most Powerful Leadership Principle

HOW TO BECOME
A SERVANT LEADER

James C. Hunter

WaterBrook
PRESS

Published by Crown Business, New York, New York.
Member of the Crown Publishing Group,
a division of Random House, Inc.
www.crownpublishing.com

This book is copublished with WaterBrook Press, 12265 Oracle Boulevard,
Suite 200, Colorado Springs, CO 80921, a division of Random House, Inc.

CROWN BUSINESS is a trademark and the Rising Sun colophon is a
registered trademark of Random House, Inc.

Published in the United States by WaterBrook Multnomah,
an imprint of the Crown Publishing Group,
a division of Random House Inc., New York.

Printed in the United States of America

Design by Karen Minster

Library of Congress Cataloging-in-Publication Data
Hunter, James C.
    The world's most powerful leadership principle : how to become a
servant leader / James C. Hunter.
    1. Leadership. 2. Leadership—Moral and ethical aspects. I. Title.
    HD57.7.H878 2004
    658.4'092—dc22   2003028103

ISBN 978-1-57856-975-5 (WaterBrook)
ISBN 978-1-4000-5334-6 (Crown)

10 9 8 7 6 5 4

2009

To the One who first taught me
that to lead is to serve.

CONTENTS

The World's
Most Powerful
Leadership
Principle

Another Leadership Book?

*People need to be reminded
more often than they need to be instructed.*

Samuel Johnson

THESE ARE NOT THE BEST OF TIMES FOR LEADERS IN corporate America.

I write this at a time when *CEO* has become a four-letter word in many circles. We are in the midst of corporate scandals involving the likes of Adelphia, Arthur Andersen, Enron, Global Crossing, Tyco, and WorldCom. Just today I read a *USA Today*/CNN/Gallup Poll stating that seven in ten Americans say they distrust CEOs of large corporations. Fully eight in ten believe top executives of large companies will take "improper actions" to help themselves at the expense of their companies. Credibility for business leaders may well be at an all-time low.

These corporate scandals leave me feeling ambivalent. On the one hand, I am pleased that corporate crooks are getting what they have coming and that the system is, at least in part, working. On the other hand, I feel sad for the many, many good, hardworking, and honest CEOs who are being painted with the same broad brush. Indeed, I have met far more honest CEOs than dishonest ones. As one pundit put it, saying all CEOs are crooks is like saying all priests are pedophiles.

WHERE ARE ALL THE LEADERS?

As an avid student and educator on the topic of leadership and specifically servant leadership, I often wonder if there is anything left to be said on the topic.

A search on Amazon.com reveals more than 280,000 titles on leadership and management! Tens of thousands of pages are written about leadership in magazines and journals each year.

Three-quarters of American corporations send people off to leadership classes each year and spend an estimated $15 *billion* on training and consulting for those on their leadership teams. Yet more than 90 percent of the leadership training and development courses organizations are spending billions on each year are a waste of time and money. Yes, the managers will receive *information* about leadership; they will probably leave the training feeling excited, warm, and fuzzy; yet less than 10 percent will actually change their behavior as a result of the training.

We have roughly 2.5 million graduated M.B.A.'s in America today, and we will graduate another 110,000 M.B.A.'s this year. Sadly, I have observed many hotshot M.B.A.'s entering organizations fresh off our nation's best campuses trying to impress everyone with how much they know, seemingly oblivious to the simple truth that people do not care what you know until they know that you care. I have met far too many M.B.A.'s who are fit to *manage* but unfit to *lead*.

Recent studies conducted by the Gallup organization show that better than two-thirds of people who leave their jobs resign because of an ineffective or incompetent manager. Put another way, the significant majority of people who leave their organization do not quit their company, they quit their *boss*.

So we arrive at a major disconnect.

With this abundance of resources directed toward developing better leaders, one could easily assume that great leaders, or at least good ones, would abound. Yet where are they? I worry that if the proverbial visitor from Mars ever arrives and demands, "Take me to your leader!" we won't have a clue where to take him (it).

It is obvious to me and to many others that something is missing.

Something very big.

YEARNING FOR MORE

In the six years since my first book, *The Servant,* an allegory about servant leadership, was published, I have been contacted what seems like countless times by people searching for ways to implement the values and principles of servant leadership in their organizations and/or personal lives. Many in leadership positions do not appear in need of any more convincing that servant leadership is the right way to lead and live, because the principles of servant leadership are self-evident. What many *are* seeking is a plan, a guidebook, or a map on how to implement the principles into their lives. They are saying, "Show me how! Tell me what I must do."

There are many in leadership positions yearning to be the leaders they know their people need and deserve. Many long to be better parents, coaches, spouses, teachers, pastors, or managers. Many in leadership positions genuinely desire alignment between their beliefs and good intentions and their actual behavior and performance.

From firsthand experience, I know there are many thousands in leadership positions who know they are failing their people and desperately desire help in developing effective leadership skills. Many have long ago recognized that the old ways of leading through command-and-control and barking orders are largely ineffective when working with a diverse workforce of 78 million baby boomers, 50 million Generation Xers, and 80 million Generation Yers, the vast majority of whom do not trust "power people."

In addition to these yearnings, there is an inward searching going on around the world, as evidenced by phenomena such as the Million Man March, Mel Gibson's movie *The Passion,* twelve-step programs, and Promise Keepers, to name just a few. Even *Business Week* magazine recently devoted its cover to a story titled "Spirituality in the Workplace." The events of September 11, 2001, have made words like *charac-*

ter, prayer, God, and *leadership* fashionable once again. I have also found in my seminars leaders looking for ways to integrate their spiritual beliefs into practical application at work and in their personal lives. The success of *The Servant* has also convinced me of that fact.

Again, it is obvious to me that people need something more.

That is why I wrote this book.

THE GOOD NEWS

The good news is that the timeless principles of servant leadership meet the tough challenges facing those in leadership positions today.

The good news is that we have the "technology" of how to become a servant leader not only in "head knowledge" but in behavior and actions as well.

The good news is that the skills of servant leadership can be learned and applied by most people who have the will and intent to change, grow, and improve.

The good news is that organizations around the world are changing their attitudes toward leadership, people, and relationships. Relational and values-based leadership has been written and talked about for decades, with great authors defining it in different ways and calling it different things. In the end, most of these folks have been talking about the same things. And that is the simple truth that leadership and life are about people and relationships. Consequently, servant leadership is emerging on a grand scale in many parts of the world. The evidence of this is that many of the most admired and successful organizations on the planet are now practicing the disciplines of servant leadership.

Fortune magazine is famous for its "lists," the most famous of which is the Fortune 500, in which American companies are rank-ordered by revenue. *Fortune* also compiles two other popular lists annually: the "100 Best Companies to Work For" and "America's Most Admired Companies."

In *Fortune*'s recent installment of the "100 Best Companies to Work For," more than one-third, thirty-five-plus organizations, are involved in the servant-leadership movement and/or specifically identify servant leadership as a core operating principle. Four of the top five on the list specifically practice servant leadership: the Container Store, Synovus Financial, TDIndustries, and Southwest Airlines.

The latest "America's Most Admired Companies" list reveals ten organizations practicing servant leadership, including well-known organizations such as Federal Express, Marriott International, Medtronic, Pella, Herman Miller, ServiceMaster, and Nestlé USA. In fact, two of the top ten "admired companies" practice servant leadership, including the planet's largest business organization, Wal-Mart, with more than $250 billion in annual sales and more than 1.4 million employees, and Southwest Airlines, one of the most successful airlines in the world.

NOW FOR THE BAD NEWS

Are you ready?

You will not become a better leader by reading this book! If you are still reading these lines after that statement, thanks for hanging in there a little longer.

Please understand that nobody ever became a better leader by reading a book, listening to an audiotape, watching a training video, or attending yet another class on leadership. You can certainly learn *about* leadership by doing those things, but you will never *become* a better leader by simply doing those things.

Becoming a skilled leader is analogous to becoming a skilled doctor, chef, lawyer, pianist, or golfer. You may gain information and insight into a subject by reading a book or sitting in a class, but application and practice is *the* key. No one ever learned to swim by reading a book.

Developing the skills of servant leadership is difficult work and comes with a price. Becoming a servant leader requires a great deal of motivation, feedback, and extended practice, as does any worthwhile discipline. Becoming a better leader is not something that is grasped intellectually, like learning algebra or how to read a balance sheet. We become leaders by applying our learning, knowledge, feedback, and experience to our everyday lives.

To become a better leader, one must be willing and motivated to change and grow. To develop leadership skills, one must be motivated to seek out and receive sometimes painful feedback from others so one can see oneself more clearly. To become a more skillful leader, one must be willing to go down deep to explore old scripts, habits, and behaviors that need to be identified and changed. To become a more effective leader, one must be motivated to break old habits and begin learning new ones. There are few things more difficult in life than breaking deep-seated habits, which is why few benefit from simply taking a class or workshop on leadership.

Most people believe that smoking can kill you over time. But that head knowledge alone has done little to dissuade the 25 percent of the population still smoking in this country. In fact, a couple of thousand people will die today, many with a cigarette still hanging in their mouth, who *know* smoking kills.

More, much more, than intellectual agreement about a certain proposition like "smoking kills" or "servant leadership is the right thing to do" is needed.

GOALS FOR THIS BOOK

My goals for this book are twofold.

My first goal is to articulate the principles of servant leadership as I have come to know and understand them in a simple, concise, and straightforward manner.

My second goal is to provide a guidebook and a map along with a simple process people can use to implement the principles of servant leadership into their lives and/or organization.

Goal #1—Clearly Defining Servant Leadership

Some may question the value of this goal, wondering if it has already been accomplished by other authors or even by my first book. In fact, what I hear most often about *The Servant* is gratitude for making a somewhat difficult topic to articulate easier to grasp.

Yet I feel compelled to redefine and rearticulate the principles of servant leadership for several reasons.

First, I am convinced that more information is needed on the powerful and timeless principles of servant leadership. Though the principles are centuries old, relatively few resources are available on the topic. A search on Amazon .com reveals a mere twenty-eight titles on servant leadership, with only a dozen or so still in print. Of those in print, the majority are directed primarily toward religious audiences.

Second, we need to be continually reminded about the basics and about doing the right thing. Think of the million-dollar athletes in spring training going over the basic fundamentals again and again. I am immersed in the world of servant leadership on an almost daily basis, yet I often find I am preaching to myself when I speak or write. I know from personal experience that we cannot hear these principles enough. I have not arrived in my development as a leader, parent, coach, or husband. I am certainly not where I want to be, but I am further along than I used to be. We need to hear the principles again and again and again; we really do need to be reminded more than we need to be instructed.

Third, *The Servant* was written seven years prior to this book being released. During that time, I have continued to be immersed in the field of servant leadership and have gleaned new insights and experiences that I am anxious to share with my readers.

Finally, writing an allegory like *The Servant* put certain constraints on how well I could express a concept or make a point and still leave the story readable and enjoyable. In this "business book" format, I have much more freedom in the way I can go about articulating these timeless principles.

If you do not desire further education on the principles of servant leadership, I would suggest you skip chapters 1 through 5 and get right into the application portion of the book, beginning in chapter 6 and continuing to the end.

Goal #2—Providing a Map for Implementation

Education in leadership principles without application is rather useless, so I intend to move from discussing servant leadership to discussing the practical application of its principles.

I often ask participants in my leadership seminars to raise their hands if they believe in continuous improvement. Virtually everyone will dutifully raise their hands in response to this question. In my hometown of Detroit, I have even had business groups sing me their organization's jingle about continuous improvement! I mean, *everyone* believes in continuous improvement these days, don't they?

I then ask how many of them believe that continuous improvement applies to them personally. Predictably, the hands will again rise.

Finally, I pose the tough question: "By definition, can you improve if you do not change?"

The audience usually looks blankly at me for a few moments before slowly shaking their heads. At this point, I will remind them of the definition of insanity: "continuing to do what you've always done and hoping for different results."

I conclude by saying, "If you all believe in continuous improvement, then each of you must, by definition, be ready and willing to change, correct?"

Of course, they will lie and say, "Yes!" in unison.

Like the weather, change is effortless to talk about, but doing something about it is another matter. Change is difficult and requires effort as we move from the familiar and comfortable to the unfamiliar and uncomfortable.

In this book, one of the primary themes is that *leadership development and character development are one*. Building character requires change and is therefore much easier said than done. The work and even the pain of changing the person we are, breaking old habits, and becoming someone different than we are today is no easy task. Let me say it again: Leadership development and character development are one. More about that later.

In this book, I will provide an uncomplicated, straightforward, three-step change process that I have seen successfully employed by literally thousands of leaders to effect change in their lives and organizations.

ARE YOU SURE YOU'RE READY FOR THIS?

Before you venture any further into this work, I strongly suggest you search the depths of your being to answer three crucial questions:

1.   Are you *truly* committed to personal continuous improvement and being a more effective leader? If your answer is yes, then you must understand and agree that personal change will be required in order to accomplish this.

2.   Can your ego handle receiving feedback, even emotionally painful feedback, from others, including subordinates, to better determine the gaps between where you are now as a leader versus where you need to be as a leader?

3.   Are you willing to do the necessary work, take the necessary risks, and suffer the necessary pain in order to close the gaps between where you currently are as a leader and where you need to be as a leader?

If your answer to any of these questions is no, there is probably no point in reading another page in this book.

If your answer to these questions is a committed yes, then this book contains some of the most significant and life-changing information you may have read in a very long time.

CHAPTER ONE

On Leadership

There are no weak platoons —
only weak leaders.

GENERAL WILLIAM CREECH

TWENTY-FIVE YEARS AGO, I BEGAN MY CAREER WORKING in the field of labor and employee relations. My territory was the same area where I was born and raised: Detroit, also known as the Motor City, the home of the American labor movement and arguably one of the toughest labor areas in the United States.

In my late twenties, I left a private company after serving as personnel director (that's what they called them back then) and became an independent labor-relations consultant working with organizations experiencing labor problems. The typical "employee problems" were union organizing drives, strikes, violence, sabotage, low morale, low commitment, high absenteeism, and excessive turnover.

As a relatively young business consultant, I felt intimidated upon entering potential client organizations. I would often find myself sitting nervously across from powerful CEOs, invariably men, sitting arrogantly behind an expensive mahogany desk, dressed to the max, and sometimes even puffing on the proverbial cigar.

They would usually begin by saying something like "We've got some pretty serious problems here, son."

Eager to please my potential clients, I would politely nod my head in agreement as I peered out their windows at the violence and the fires burning down below.

"Yes, sir," I would reply, trying to sound confident and self-assured. "We do seem to have some problems here. I think we should begin by . . ."

As if not hearing a word I said, they would interrupt with "Let me tell you what we need to do here, son" and then proceed to tell me what "the problem was," followed by, of course, the solution to the problem. These egomaniacs always had everything figured out. It made me wonder why they even called me in.

"Our problem is that troublemaker named Chucky out there driving the forklift, the bigmouth handing out the union cards. Once we shut him up, our problems will be solved, everyone will be happy here, and we will be back to business as usual!" Chucky on the forklift, or Norma Jean in the warehouse, or Bill in customer service. I discovered over the years that everyone seemed to have a "Chucky on the forklift" who needed to be "fixed," and all of our problems would be solved.

And I used to believe it! I would think, "No wonder you're the CEO and making the big bucks. What a brilliant idea!"

So I spent several seasons running around organizations trying to silence the Chuckys of the world. I even have some scars to prove it.

Over time, I came to the surprising conclusion that Chucky was not the problem. In fact, Chucky was usually the only person in the place telling the truth! It even got to the point that when I entered a dysfunctional organization, I asked specifically to speak to Chucky so I could figure out what the heck was really going on! I sure wasn't going to find out in the front office. They were generally clueless up there.

Over time, I became convinced that 9.5 times out of 10 when I entered a dysfunctional organization, first day, first interview, talking to the big dog in the big chair, I was speaking directly to the problem.

In order to face myself in the mirror each morning, I felt compelled to tell the leader that he was paying me well to address the *symptoms* but not the *problem*. So I would conduct a dog-and-pony show over a couple of weeks to earn the right to tell the leader that he was the problem. As you can probably surmise, a few assignments were cut short following those conversations.

My wife is a psychologist who has also dealt with organizations for many years, namely marriages and families. Any time two or more people are gathered together for a purpose, an organization exists and there is an opportunity for leadership.

In her practice, parents often bring in their children pleading, "You've got to fix these kids! These kids are acting out terribly!"

Early in her career as a "neophyte shrink," Denise would accept the assessment of the parents and begin "fixing the kids" while the parents went off to dinner. In short order, she came to the same conclusion I had—namely, that the problem invariably resides in the leadership team, not in the expressed symptoms being acted out in the organization. Now the kids go off to the playroom while she goes to work on the parents.

There is another phenomenon that occurs in our respective businesses. We both tend to work with the extremes of very dysfunctional organizations and very healthy organizations—organizations or individuals with such severe symptoms that they must reach out for help and organizations or individuals that are "doing quite well, thank you" but want an even better edge as they strive for continuous improvement and being the best they can be.

We have observed a similarity between healthy organizations and unhealthy organizations, healthy marriages and unhealthy marriages, healthy churches and unhealthy churches, healthy families and dysfunctional families. And the similarity revolves around leadership. We have found the single greatest predictor of organizational health or dysfunction to be leadership or lack thereof.

About fifteen years ago, I made a decision to stop trying to fix the symptoms and begin focusing on the root of the problem. I have been teaching the principles of servant leadership ever since.

"Everything rises and falls on leadership."

"It all starts at the top."

"No weak platoons, only weak leaders."

Could there actually be something to these old clichés?

LEADERSHIP IN OUR INSTITUTIONS

In my travels in the corporate world, I am troubled when I observe far too many "managers" concerned about doing things the right way and looking good for their boss rather than striving to do the right thing for the people they lead.

I look at our great nation's capital and see many of our elected politicians analyzing polling data and making political calculations based upon what people *want* rather than providing leadership and seeking to give their constituents what they *need*. Mercifully, there is evidence this may be changing in a post–September 11 world. As President Harry S. Truman put it, "How far would Moses have gone if he had taken a poll in Egypt?"

I observe far too many parents attempting to be "best buddy" to their children by running around trying to gratify their never-ending wants rather than providing the leadership they need. Leadership that provides boundaries, love, feedback, and discipline that children so desperately *need* to be the best they can be. I see parents more concerned with spoiling and lavishing upon their children the material things they themselves did *not* receive growing up while failing to provide them with the important things they *did* receive from their parents.

I encounter far too many professionals in our educational institutions who see their roles primarily as imparting book knowledge to a "bunch of kids" they don't really care much for. They are more interested in rushing to get everything "covered" before the semester ends rather than seeing themselves in leadership roles with the responsibility of serving their students and assisting them in developing their character, so necessary in order to live a successful life. Theodore Roosevelt said it best: "To educate a person in mind but not in morals is to educate a menace to society." We must never forget that the horrors of Nazi Germany arose from the educated and refined land of Nietzsche, Beethoven, Einstein, and Mercedes-Benz.

I observe coaches intent upon winning at all costs rather than mentoring and leading our young people in their character development, utilizing the great metaphors athletics can provide.

I know leaders in churches and synagogues who appear more concerned with the weekly head count and budget considerations than in providing the leadership their congregations need most. I observe religious leaders more intent on saying the things people *want* to hear rather than having the moral courage to say the things they *need* to hear for fear of upsetting them, resulting in their withholding contributions and/or support.

In short, I observe far too many in leadership positions failing to do the right thing for those they lead. Too often, leaders are taking the path of least resistance and trying to "avoid the hassle."

This widespread lack of leadership is a failure of character, which is why leadership has everything to do with character. Character is about doing the right thing. Leadership is about doing the right thing. It has even been suggested that managers do things right while leaders do the right thing.

The good news is that we can all choose to do something about our character. In fact, we can choose to grow our character until leadership and doing the right thing become second nature.

LEADERSHIP DEFINED

In *The Servant,* I defined leadership as:

> **The skill of influencing people to enthusiastically work toward goals identified as being for the common good.**

Over the past several years, I have modified this definition somewhat as my knowledge and experience in leadership has been evolving.

Today, I define leadership as:

> The *skills* of *influencing* people to enthusiastically work toward goals identified as being for the common good, with *character* that inspires confidence.

The operative words in this definition are *skills, influencing,* and *character,* which will be explored later.

But before we go there, let's explore what leadership is *not*.

LEADERSHIP IS NOT MANAGEMENT

When conducting leadership seminars, I often begin by saying, "I am going to level the playing field right from the start this morning. My basic assumption will be that you are all excellent managers, have solid technical abilities, and are skilled at accomplishing tasks. I will give each of you an A-plus in management skills right out of the chute this morning.

"In fact, chances are you rose to a position of leadership in your organization by being proficient at those things. If you came to hear about being a better manager today, you are in the wrong room. Today, we are going to talk about leadership, not management."

Management is about the things we do: the planning, the budgeting, the organizing, the problem-solving, being in control, maintaining order, developing strategies, and a host of other *things*. Management is what we *do*. Leadership is who we *are*.

I have known many great managers who were train wrecks when it came to leading other human beings and inspiring them to do great things. Conversely, I have known some highly effective leaders who were not particularly astute managers. Few have ever accused Winston Churchill, FDR, or Ronald Reagan of being a good manager.

"Good managers" often have a style that is authoritative and command-and-control because they mistakenly believe they must have all the answers, fix all of the problems, and, above all else, maintain control. Most leadership training, if they receive any at all, is simply more management training turning out people capable of managing things but not producing people capable of leading and inspiring others to action.

Simply knowing how to do the job well has little to do with developing the skills necessary to inspire *others* to do the job well. The technical and task-oriented skills that managers work so hard to develop and that have served them well in rising to leadership positions do not serve them well in becoming effective leaders. A whole different skill set is required.

Leadership involves getting people from the neck up. Leadership is influencing people to contribute their hearts, minds, spirits, creativity, and excellence and to give their all for their team. Leadership is getting people to commit to the mission, to take the hill, to be all they can be.

When Ross Perot ran for president in 1992, he made a great statement that I will paraphrase: You do not manage people; if you want something to manage, go manage your inventory, your checkbook, or yourself.

You do not manage people.

You *lead* people.

LEADERSHIP IS NOT ABOUT BEING THE BOSS

In America, we all too often confuse good businesspeople with good leaders. A successful businessperson does not define a successful leader. Observes famous investor Warren Buffett, "I've seen a lot of not-very-good human beings succeed in business. I wish it were otherwise."

The media loves to idolize and demonize successful businesspeople of our day and glorify them on the covers of magazines. Business "leaders" are often defined as great visionaries, strategic planners, organizational gurus, and tactical geniuses. These may be important management skills, but they have little to do with excellent leadership and influencing people to give their all to the mission.

This tendency to glorify and complicate leadership only serves to make leadership more remote and seemingly unattainable to the average supervisor, parent, coach, pastor, or teacher out there in the trenches trying to lead his or her group of rather stubborn and defiant Generation Xers.

Please note that one does *not* have to be in charge of others or in a position of power to meet the criteria of our definition of leadership. We have all met people in organizations with little or no positional power who daily influence others to be more enthusiastic, more committed, and more willing to be the best they can be. Again, one of the operative words in our leadership definition is the ability to *influence* others for good.

It has been said that truly effective teams are never led by dictators or autocrats. It has even been suggested that genuine communities are leader*less,* but it is probably more accurate to say that the most effective teams are groups of all leaders in which everyone is taking *personal* responsibility for the success of their team. Indeed, anyone who ever said marriage was 50/50 probably was not married for long. A successful marriage, like any successful organization, is 100/100 and requires the players to get their heads fully in the game. Everyone on the team is influencing others and leaves their mark on the team. The only question is what kind of mark each member will leave behind.

I witnessed this principle recently while traveling on Southwest Airlines. As mentioned earlier, Southwest is a servant-leadership organization and is listed on the New York Stock Exchange under the ticker symbol LUV. One of its famous slogans is "The airline that love built."

Living near Detroit means I travel Northwest Airlines almost exclusively because Detroit is a Northwest hub. On a business trip two years ago, I had the good fortune of getting bumped off Northwest and ended up with a ticket on Southwest. I was excited by this because I had heard the stories of the company's servant leadership and of the flight attendants doing crazy things like hiding in overhead compartments and pulling practical jokes on passengers. I was eager to see if any of this servant-leadership stuff on Southwest was really true.

I checked in and received my plastic boarding card. I remember being a bit surprised that there was no seat assignment on the card when suddenly somebody yelled, "Go!"

Not being skilled in this new way of boarding an airplane, I got pushed and shoved around until I ended up in the back row in a middle seat. To say the least, I was not too impressed.

Just before the cabin door was closed for departure, a preteen boy jumped onto the plane, his arms filled with large boxes of candy, the type sold by schoolchildren for fund-raisers.

There may have been one or two empty seats left on the plane, and the overhead-storage availability had long been depleted. As a very frequent flyer, I have been around my share of crabby and less-than-helpful flight attendants, and I was sure this kid was going to get blasted with the usual "Those boxes will need to be checked below! Can't you see we are out of room back here?"

But that is not what happened.

Instead, this young flight attendant asked the boy if he would like assistance in selling his candy. Of course, the boy's eyes lit up as he said, "Sure."

The flight attendant then proceeded to take the candy and put it into the cockpit with the pilots! I had never seen a flight attendant put a passenger's belongings into the cockpit before, nor have I since that day.

The next thing I knew, we were at cruising altitude, and the flight attendant was on the overhead PA system announcing that candy bars were going to be passed down the aisle for $2 per bar. The flight attendant concluded the announcement by saying that she wanted to know who would be the first person *not* to buy one so she could inform the rest of the passengers to stay clear of the grump in seat 10C! The plane roared with laughter.

Of course, the candy was gone before the boxes reached the halfway point in the fuselage. The flight attendant then had to deal with the cranky passengers who did *not* get a chance to buy some candy! One guy yelled across the aisle and offered $5 over the selling price to another guy, who flatly refused him. I mean, we had eBay going on right in the aisles at thirty-seven thousand feet! I am not kidding you: The whole plane was involved in this thing!

That was an act of leadership on the part of one flight attendant who had no positional power in her company. She went the extra mile with that boy and *influenced* that entire airplane! I am sure I was not the only one on that airplane who would never forget the look on that boy's face as he held the empty boxes and a thick wad of cash.

My experiences with Southwest Airlines since that day have been consistent in this regard. Whenever I fly that airline, I continually find a group of people working together to do whatever is necessary to accomplish the mission, including influencing the customers and one another. On many occasions, I have watched as this "group of all leaders" do whatever is necessary to make the flight successful, including encouraging one another, pushing one another, utilizing humor, working enthusiastically, and so on. Doing whatever is necessary to get people to be the best they can be. Doing whatever is necessary to *influence* the customers' experience.

Now, some could try to dismiss Southwest as a wacky, off-the-wall, flaky organization, *except* for the fact that Southwest is arguably the most successful airline in America, if not the world, today. In a highly unionized industry, one in which it is difficult to be profitable, Southwest has not had an unprofitable year in more than thirty years, including the nearly three years since September 11, 2001, which have been disastrous for the airline industry.

And some could try to write Southwest off as an aberration, *except* for the fact that Southwest's market capitalization as I pen these words is $11 billion, nearly two *times* the market capitalization of the "Big Six" U.S.-based airlines *combined,* which includes American, United, Delta, Northwest, Continental, and US Airways.

When an organization is successful in getting its members to take leadership responsibility, to understand that *everyone* is responsible for the success of the team, it is an awesome sight to behold. Unfortunately, this largely untapped resource lies dormant in most of the organizations in the world. Thankfully, there are signs that this is changing.

Again, one need not have positional power in order to positively influence others. We all leave our mark on the organizations we choose to become a part of. The only question is, what kind of mark will we leave?

With that said, I want to clarify that for the purposes of this work, I will generally be speaking about those in traditional positions of leadership within their organizations who have the customary responsibilities of the growth, development, and performance of those they lead.

Let me further add to our definition of leadership by stating what leadership *is*.

LEADERSHIP IS AN AWESOME RESPONSIBILITY

Reflect for a moment on all of the different leadership roles for which people "sign up" in their lifetime: manager, spouse, parent, coach, teacher, clergy, and many, many more.

Never forget: When we "signed up" to be the leader, we volunteered for an awesome responsibility. Human beings have been entrusted to our care, and much is at stake. I never cease to be amazed at how casually and nonchalantly people approach their leadership roles.

I keep saying "signed up," because we are all leadership volunteers. Presumably, nobody coerces us to marry, forces us to be parents, or makes us take a paycheck from the stockholder or taxpayer every other week. We signed up for these tours of duty. We come freely, and we are free to leave. The point is, we signed up for something big—and something very important.

Think about the role of a manager in an organization. Employees will spend half of their waking hours living and working in an environment created by this manager. Employees will spend more waking time with this manager and one another than they will with their families.

Further, this manager has been entrusted with the careers of other people. Think of that! Will these people grow and develop as a result of the leader's influence? Will they be better human beings as a result of having contact with this leader? Will they be inspired to do the right thing and develop their character? Indeed, the ultimate test of leadership is this: Are the people better off when they leave than when they got there?

Think about the awesome responsibility of being a parent. As a kid, I'm stuck with you for the rest of my life! I can't get away from that. Do you think that's a big responsibility, Mom? Who about you, Dad?

How about a teacher, pastor, coach, rabbi? Ever had a person influence you positively or negatively for life? I have. As leaders, we need to reflect for a moment on the impact we are having on other people and the responsibility inherent in this position of trust.

How we behave as the boss at work today affects what goes on around the dinner table in other people's homes tonight. Anyone who has ever had a bad boss can certainly relate to what I am talking about. As Max Depree, author of *Leadership Is an Art* and *Leadership Jazz,* is fond of saying, "Leadership . . . is a serious meddling in the lives of others."

I believe this is where servant leadership begins. We need to reflect regularly on this awesome responsibility for which we signed up and recognize that our choices and behaviors are impacting lives. I have found that getting people to reflect upon the awesome responsibility inherent in their leadership roles is an important first step toward growth and change.

Many years ago, I had a friend tell me that he believed being an ordained pastor was a "high calling." I agreed but said I also believed being a supervisor was a "high calling." Just think how one manager can positively or negatively influence the lives of others simply by how he or she behaves on a daily basis. Says basketball coaching legend John Wooden, "A leader . . . has a most powerful influence on those he or she leads, perhaps more than anyone outside of the family. . . . I consider it a sacred trust."

LEADERSHIP IS A SKILL

Are leaders born, or are leaders made?

The age-old question.

"My grandpa was a lousy supervisor, so that is why I am a lousy supervisor," or "My mama was a poor wife and mother, and that's why I'm a poor wife and mother. I just didn't get those leadership genes in my DNA strands."

Is leadership genetic? Is leadership merely a series of molecular, self-replicating materials that are the main constituent of chromosomes either present or absent in your genetic makeup?

Management guru Peter Drucker flatly states that while there may be some "born leaders," there are surely too few to depend on them. "Leadership is something that must be learned."

Adds Warren Bennis, "The most dangerous leadership myth is that leaders are born — that there is a genetic factor to leadership. This myth asserts that people simply either have certain charismatic qualities or not. That's nonsense; in fact, the opposite is true. Leaders are made rather than born."

Whether they are born or made is a crucial point because if we believe leadership is a set of traits we are born with or without, then we do not have to take responsibility for it. We can just blame our ancestors. Once we accept the fact that leadership is a skill, we're on the hook. What are we doing to develop that skill to the best of our ability?

Twenty-five years ago, I wasn't so sure leadership was a skill. I believed that effective leadership was some combination of genetic and environmental factors, mixed in with a strong personality and a good education. A dozen years ago, I started to become convinced that leadership was a skill as I watched myself and others I knew develop the skill through education and application. Today, after watching hundreds of committed managers grow and become more effective leaders, there is no doubt in my mind that leadership is a skill — that is, a learned or acquired ability. Indeed, I now *know* that the vast majority of the population can develop the skills of leadership.

In addition, with the high probability that virtually

everyone will assume one or more traditional leadership roles in their lifetime as parents, spouses, managers, coaches, teachers, et cetera, I have a difficult time believing that the good Lord would reserve the essential skills necessary to being an effective leader to those fortunate few blessed with just the right DNA composition.

In his bestselling book, *Good to Great,* Jim Collins discusses the highest performing leaders in the truly great companies and refers to them as "Level 5" leaders. Says Mr. Collins, "I believe that potential Level 5 leaders exist all around us, if we just know what to look for, and that many people have the potential to evolve into Level 5."

I do believe there are people incapable of becoming effective leaders, but I believe the percentage is less than 10 percent. This small group would include those suffering from severe personality or character disorders and other serious mental or emotional deficiencies who may not have the raw material necessary to develop or sustain healthy relationships with other human beings.

Barring serious mental or emotional deficiencies, I am convinced that the seeds of leadership are present and available to the vast majority of the population. Leadership is a latent skill waiting to be developed in most people.

Robert Greenleaf, noted consultant, lecturer, and author, wrote about servant leadership decades before it became fashionable in business circles. He recognized this latent leadership potential when he wrote, "Many, many teachers at both secondary and college levels have sufficient latitude in dealing with their students that they could, on their own, help nurture the servant-leader potential that, I believe, is latent to some degree in almost every young person."

My dictionary defines a skill as "a learned or acquired ability." If leadership is a skill, that definition would certainly imply that it is available to most people. As stated earlier, developing leadership skills is analogous to developing other skills such as learning to shoot baskets, play the piano, hit a golf ball, or fly an airplane. To be sure, not everyone can play basketball like Michael Jordan, play piano like George Winston, play golf like Tiger Woods, or fly an airplane like Chuck Yeager. Nevertheless, most of the population *could* become more skilled at shooting baskets, playing the piano, hitting a golf ball, or flying an airplane than they are today. Certainly, it would take a lot of motivation, extended practice, and discipline. But we could drastically improve our skills in nearly any area if we combined proper desire, proper tools, and proper actions.

Similarly, developing leadership skills may not mean we will be able to lead General Motors or the United States of America anytime soon, but everyone can be the best leader he or she is capable of becoming.

Our past choices define the leader we are today and may define the leader we will be tomorrow—but not necessarily. We can *choose* to develop the skill of leadership. We can choose to further develop our character. We can choose to be someone different in the future than we are today.

SAYING IT'S SO DOESN'T MAKE IT SO

Most of the decision-makers I meet in organizations today *say* they believe leadership to be a skill set but behave as if they do not really believe it.

The evidence clearly shows that the vast majority of managers in this country are promoted into leadership positions with little or no training in how to effectively lead their organizations' most valuable resource and asset — that is, its people. All too often, people get promoted because "She's great with the numbers," or "He's a good soldier," or "He's as loyal as they come." It has become a broken record in far too many organizations. We promote our best salesperson to be the sales manager, and now we've lost our best salesperson and we've got a lousy leader!

Most every executive I have ever met has told me emphatically that employees are an organization's most valuable asset. If that were *really* true, would they just hire or promote "loyal" or "good numbers" people to lead and service this great asset? Hardly. Yet this is precisely how most organizations behave. They hire or promote people into leadership positions, send them to a daylong "supervisory skills" seminar, touch them with their magic wand, and then turn them loose! Recent studies suggest that spot training can actually have a *negative* impact on leadership performance.

Again, once we accept the fact that leadership is a skill, we have the responsibility to see to it that we are developing those skills. If we are decision-makers in an organization, we have a responsibility, even a moral obligation, to ensure that our greatest assets are properly cared for and that the members of the leadership team have all the tools they need to succeed in their awesome responsibility as leaders.

LEADERSHIP IS INFLUENCE

One Minute Manager author Ken Blanchard states, "What is leadership? It's an influence process."

Leadership is influencing people to willingly, even enthusiastically, contribute their hearts, minds, creativity, excellence, and other resources toward mutually beneficial goals. Leadership is influencing people to commit to the mission. Leadership is influencing people to become the best they are capable of becoming. Accordingly, leadership is *not* synonymous with management. Leadership is synonymous with influence.

In the old days, he who knew the most about the company's technology or was the best manager got to be king. Not so anymore. You now regularly see top executives of Fortune 500 companies switching industries. Lou Gerstner, CEO during IBM's dramatic turnaround, previously made cookies at Nabisco; the CEO of Burger King used to run Northwest Airlines; the leader of Home Depot ran the power-systems division at General Electric. In fact, many excellent organizations these days are "hiring for character, training for skill."

Leadership is somewhat analogous to being the conductor of an orchestra. We can teach you music theory and how to play a musical instrument. But who has the skill to get a variety of different people playing different instruments to align and play the music in harmony? Who can influence others to play with their heads in the game? Who brings *that* skill to the party?

Let me give you an example of leading through influence. Herb Kelleher, the recently retired CEO of Southwest Airlines, once sent a memo to his employees informing them that the company was about to have an unprofitable quarter. In that memo, he asked each of them to save $5 a day. It didn't matter if you were flying the airplanes, serving the coffee, or changing the tires. Everyone needed to pull together and save $5 per day. He signed the memo, "LUV, Herb."

Southwest Airlines cut 5.6 percent from its operating expenses that quarter, a huge amount that allowed the company to be profitable.

That is leadership. When he spoke, he had his people from the neck up. How many CEOs do you know who could ask the masses to save $5 a day? You can almost hear the "Yeah, whatever!" as they crumple the memo and throw it in the trash or even on the floor.

John Maxwell, the prolific leadership author, sums up leadership by saying, "Leadership is influence—nothing more and nothing less."

LEADERSHIP IS ABOUT CHARACTER

Life is a series of choices we face daily, and you and I have made hundreds of choices today. I read that one psychologist estimated that the average person makes fifteen thousand choices in the average day.

Now, I am not talking about what color shoes or underwear we choose to wear or where we will have lunch today. I'm talking about the hundreds of choices we make daily about how we will behave toward the people who will cross our paths. I am talking about choices of character.

You know, choices like: Will I be patient or impatient? Kind or unkind? Puffed up, boastful, and arrogant, or humble? Respectful or disrespectful? Selfless or selfish? Forgiving or unforgiving? Honest or dishonest? Committed or just involved?

Remember Psych 101 with Pavlov's dogs and stimulus-and-response? There is a small world of choice between the stimulus we face in life and the response we choose to make to the stimulus coming at us. This little world is the world we must get ahold of if we aspire to be more effective leaders and better human beings.

And there is a lot of stimuli coming at us, isn't there? Bills, bosses, retirement planning, health issues, childrens' college education to plan for, rude and intolerant people, and on and on. Yet we have the power to choose our response to any stimulus. One person goes to Vietnam, loses his arm and legs, returns home, and burns out on heroin. Another person goes to Vietnam and loses those same limbs, yet returns home and serves as the United States senator from Georgia. Same stimulus, different response.

In fact, the older I get, the more I am convinced that

life is not so much what happens to us as it is how we respond to what happens to us.

This world between stimulus and response is the world of character. Character is our moral maturity and commitment to doing the right thing regardless of the personal costs. Character involves the will to respond to stimuli according to values and principles rather than to appetites, urges, whims, or impulses. We are not animals.

Remember, leadership is character in action, and leadership development and character development are one. Character is doing the right thing. Leadership is doing the right thing. Chapter 7 is devoted to the topic of character and how we build it.

THE ULTIMATE TEST

The true test of the effectiveness of the leader is this: Are your people better off when they leave than when they arrived?

Are your children going to be effective human beings, capable of being loving parents, capable of leading and serving others? Are your employees more employable, better people, and have they grown more as a result of your leadership and influence? As a wise general put it, "The first duty of any leader is to create more leaders."

In his 1970 essay "The Servant as Leader," Robert Greenleaf summed this point up by saying: "Do those served grow as persons? Do they, while being served, become healthier, wiser, freer, more autonomous, more likely themselves to become servants?"

Remember, the leader always leaves his or her mark. The only question is what type of mark is left behind. Are people better or worse off because the leader was there?

Larry Bossidy, former CEO of AlliedSignal and coauthor of *Execution: The Discipline of Getting Things Done,* puts it this way: "You won't remember when you retire what you did in the first quarter of 1994, or the third. What you'll remember is how many people you developed. How many people you helped have a better career because of your interest and your dedication to their development. . . . When confused as to how you're doing as a leader, find out how the people you lead are doing. You'll know the answer."

IS SERVANT LEADERSHIP FOR WIMPS?

In my travels, I find many in leadership positions who are skeptical about servant leadership because they believe it to be some sort of namby-pamby, warm and fuzzy, passive style of leadership. Many skeptics get a horrific mental image of inverting the organizational pyramid and "turning the asylum over to the inmates."

Servant leadership is anything but that.

Servant leaders can be very "pyramid" minded, even autocratic, when it comes to certain aspects of running an organization. Aspects like the mission (where are we headed?), values (what are the rules of the house governing behavior on our journey?), standards (how will we define and measure excellence?), and accountability (what happens if there are gaps between standards and performance?). The great servant leaders I've known can be quite dictatorial when it comes to *those* issues.

Servant leadership does not allow one to abdicate his or her leadership responsibility to define the mission, set the rules governing behavior, set standards, and define accountability. The servant leader does not commission a poll, conduct a committee meeting, or have a democratic vote to determine the answers to these questions. Indeed, people look to the leader to provide this direction.

However, once this direction has been provided, it becomes time to turn the organizational structure upside down and help people win! The leadership now becomes responsive to those being led by identifying and meeting their legitimate needs so they can become the best they are capable of becoming and effectively accomplish the stated mission.

CHAPTER TWO

On Power and Authority

*The value of coercive power
is inverse to its use.*

ROBERT GREENLEAF

"IN THIS WORLD NOTHING IS CERTAIN BUT DEATH AND taxes," Benjamin Franklin once declared.

Not true, Mr. Franklin!

There are people in the United States today living communally in the woods up in the Pacific Northwest who do not even use money, let alone pay taxes. How do you pay taxes if you do not use money?

The only two certainties in life are death and *choices*. Søren Kierkegaard, the Danish philosopher, pointed out that not making a choice is, itself, a choice.

The quality of our lives, leadership, and character are determined by the quality of our daily choices.

When we signed up to be the leader, we made the first choice. Now, as the leader, we have to make another choice: Are we going to lead by power or through authority?

The vast majority of traditional leadership roles comes prepackaged with power. But relatively few leaders ever develop the authority to accompany the power with which they have been entrusted.

Power and authority. What is the difference?

POWER DEFINED

If you have ever taken a class in sociology, you will probably recognize the name of Max Weber, one of the founders of that field of study. Almost a hundred years ago, Weber wrote a book entitled *The Theory of Social and Economic Organization*, in which he articulated the differences between power and authority, and we still use these definitions widely today.

Power is the ability to force or coerce others to do your will, even if they would choose not to, because of your position or your might. A simple paraphrase of Weber's definition of power would be "Do it or else!" If I have the ability to spank you, bomb you, beat you up, write you up, or fire you, I can compel you to do my will.

As one of my favorite Gestapo-style managers loves to bark, "It's a power world, baby!"

AUTHORITY DEFINED

Authority, on the other hand, is something quite different than power. Authority is the *skill*—there's that word again— of getting others *willingly* to do your will because of your personal influence. A simple paraphrase of Weber's definition of authority would be "I'll do it for *you*."

Another way to look at power and authority is this. Power can be bought and sold, given and taken away. Just because you happen to be my sister-in-law, I can put you in a position of power by appointing you vice president. If you were born with the right genes, you get to be the prince. If you inherit the most money, you get to be the largest shareholder. History is littered with clueless rulers, czars, and managers.

Not so with authority. Authority is never bought or sold, never given or taken away. Authority is about who you are as a person. *You* inspire me, the person that you *are*. Authority is about your character.

One of the themes of this book is that legitimate leadership must be built upon authority. To develop this theme, let's examine power and its use in a little more depth.

POWER AND RELATIONSHIPS

Let there be no mistake: Power works.

If I tell my child to take out the garbage or my employee to write that report or there will be heck to pay, the job will probably get done. Power does work, and one can get a few seasons out of power. However, there is a downside to power—a rather major downside.

The downside of power is that it damages relationships.

If you power your children or spouse around, over time you will begin to see some nasty symptoms arise. My wife spent a large part of her counseling career dealing with those symptoms.

If you power your employees around, soon you will see some nasty little behaviors start coming out of the walls on you. I spent one-half of my consulting career dealing with those symptoms in organizations, including strikes, violence, sabotage, union drives, turnover, absenteeism, low commitment, low morale — pick your symptom. The "kids" will start acting out all over the place.

The United States military learned this decades ago. They will put you in boot camp with some screaming drill instructor, but only for a season, perhaps six or eight weeks. Then they put you in a squadron or platoon headed up by a leader. Why? Because over time power begins to damage relationships.

RELATIONSHIPS AND BUSINESS

Believe it or not, I have had people say to me, "We are in the automobile-supply industry. What do damaged relationships have to do with my business?"

Everything.

No matter what product or service your organization produces, you are in the relationship business. Have you figured this out yet? It took me twenty years to understand that all life is — all business is — is a series of relationships. Without people, there is no business.

In my leadership seminars, I often ask, "Why does your organization exist?"

Of course, I get the usual "To make a profit!" response, sometimes even shouted out in unison.

At that point, I will bang the table, make a loud buzzer noise, and shout, "Wrong answer! That's not why your organization exists, but thank you for playing!"

I go on to explain that the only reason *any* organization exists is because it meets a human need. When your organization fails to meet those needs or your competition meets those needs better than you do, you will no longer exist. Profit is an essential component of a healthy organization, but it is not why an organization *exists*. An analogy would be life itself. We must have oxygen (profit) to survive, but it is not why we exist.

Healthy organizations consist of healthy relationships between customers, employees, owners (shareholders, taxpayers, etc.), and significant others such as vendors, suppliers, the community, unions, and the government. Healthy relationships, healthy business; bad relationships, bad business.

How does one go about developing healthy relationships with these groups? By identifying and meeting their legitimate needs. Serving them. Not by doing what they want and being slaves — rather, by providing what they need for the long-term interests of all.

We have been slowly discovering over the past thirty years or so that the power style of management gives rise to nasty collateral activities, including head games, adversarialism, low trust, cronyism, political games, and a host of other unhealthy behaviors damaging to relationships and consequently damaging to the organization. Excessive command-

and-control styles create fear and undermine trust, which ultimately destroys relationships and growth.

A power culture in the new millennium is simply unable to compete with a culture of excellence, speed, quality, innovation—in short, with a culture in which people are playing with their heads in the game. A power culture literally sucks the life "spirit" out of an organization.

OLD PARADIGMS

As I travel to different parts of the world teaching the principles of servant leadership, I have little difficulty getting audiences excited and bought into the concepts and principles involved. Indeed, the principles are self-evident. The difficulty lies not in getting people excited about the new things but in getting people to let go of the old things—namely, the paradigms they operate from.

In my previous book, I devoted an entire chapter to paradigms and the influence our paradigms have over us. When it comes to leadership, many of us are saddled with old ideas and models that perhaps once served a useful purpose but may not be a good model for leading employees in a new and ever-changing world.

The old command-and-control "power" style of leadership has been around for thousands of years and is alive and well today. They built the great pyramids in Egypt using power, and this style of leadership has been used in most organizations around the world ever since. I wonder: Were the great pyramids built to honor the pyramid style of management?

After our great successes in World War I and World War II, many Americans assumed that the military pyramid style was the best way to run *any* organization, and it was therefore transferred into most organizations. In the home: Dad at the top, Mom in the middle, and then the kids at the bottom, although this has changed to a large degree in our country in the past couple of decades. In the church: pope at the top; then cardinals, bishops, priests; and finally the laity. In organizations: CEO at the top; then VPs, managers, supervisors; and finally, at the bottom, what we in our enlightened age now call "associates."

Of course, the world was much different immediately after World War II than it is today. Most of the civilized world from Europe to Asia had been bombed to ruins, and consequently we in the United States had little competition for our products and services. The United States reigned supreme in the global marketplace and could do little wrong, a simple enough task when there is little or no competition.

Power appeared to work splendidly in the workplace for the first couple of postwar decades. The rule of management was "I don't want you to think—I want you to just do what I say!" (Translation: I want you from the neck down.) "When I want your opinion I'll give it to you!" The Mushroom Theory of Management was the rage, with its motto, "Keep your employees in the dark, and throw lots of manure on them." Many managers could relate to the characters in the movie *Love Story*—because being the boss meant never having to say you're sorry.

The true belief about people in the workplace was well expressed by a term often used to describe employees: "hired hands." Henry Ford summed up this paradigm when he said, "Why is it I always get the whole person when all I really want is a pair of hands?

In a pyramid culture, the inertia of the organization looks upward to making the boss happy and being responsive to what he or she wants. Jack Welch, former CEO of General Electric, has noted that when employees are "looking up the food chain worshipping the king and queen," they've turned their back ends to the customer.

In a pyramid culture, people get promoted according to their technical or functional expertise or because they are "good soldiers." And even worse, in this culture people are often promoted to their level of incompetence, a practice dubbed the Peter Principle. The assumption, of course, is that people who are technically strong or can do the job best can get others to do the job well by telling them how to do it.

How ridiculous! Just because a person can do the job well does not mean that he or she can inspire and influence others to do the job well. A new way of thinking and a new and different skill set are required. As Albert Einstein put it, "You cannot achieve a new goal by applying the same level of thinking that got you where you are today."

Task-oriented, technically or functionally strong employees promoted to leadership positions face another barrier. In the past, they often felt good when they left work at night because of all the "things" they accomplished or all the "fires" they put out.

In a leadership position, the measuring stick of success changes. Efforts made to do right by people, deposits made in emotional bank accounts, or efforts made in coaching, teaching, and encouraging people may not show fruit for weeks, months, even years. This can be very difficult for people who are used to immediate gratification and quantifiable results at the end of the day. So they often resort to what they know best to get results: "Do it this way and do it now!"

We would laugh at a farmer who planted his crop in November and then complained that the fruit failed to arrive before the snow came. With leadership, there is no cramming for finals. Leadership requires that we develop the essential life skills of delaying gratification and being patient, trusting in the law of the harvest and having faith that if we do our part the fruit will come. We must be willing to bear the trial of not knowing when the fruit will arrive or even if the fruit will ever be evident in some people. This can be very difficult for task-minded managers who want results *now*.

With this in mind, it should be no mystery why the world is littered with so many bad bosses.

OOPS, THE WORLD CHANGED

There is an old saying in the Far East: "When the gods wish to destroy us, they first give us forty years of prosperity."

For a few decades, nobody could really argue with the unparalleled success that American business was enjoying domestically and internationally. The pyramid style of management must have been working! We could do no wrong.

Then the world changed. Many of the countries that had been defeated and largely destroyed began to rebuild and were soon challenging America in the marketplace. Before long, German, Japanese, Korean, and other fierce competitors were beating the United States in the marketplace by whipping us in efficiency, quality, and service. Japanese management, through team concepts, quality initiatives, kaizan, kanban, just-in-time, and other programs, showed us how important it was to get people from the neck up. Neck down was no longer good enough.

Thankfully, by the late 1970s, many organizations in America began to wake up.

Many other organizations have yet to wake up.

POWER CAN BE EXPENSIVE

And the world continues to change.

In today's world, having power-style managers running an organization can be very costly.

These are the days of *Oprah,* twelve-step programs, protecting our inner child, and standing up for our rights. These are the days when people do not take matters into their own hands — they take 'em to court!

Employment litigation is exploding nationwide, charging

harassment, defamation, battery, intentional infliction of emotional distress, discrimination, and abusive and hostile work environments. Indeed, every state in America recognizes some form of the common law of intentional infliction of emotional distress, which is a frequent companion claim made in discrimination and harassment suits. Infliction-of-emotional-distress claims generally involve conduct that is intentional and offensive to generally accepted standards of behavior and causes severe emotional distress. Out-of-control managers can even be personally sued.

According to Jury Verdict Research, the median compensatory-damage award for employment suits is $150,000. Compensatory damages do *not* include attorney fees, and the loser often must pay plaintiff *and* defendant attorney fees, which run $50,000 to $80,000 per side in typical suits. Even more scary, compensatory damages are separate from punitive damages, which can be astronomical.

Having "offensive conduct" being defined by a sympathetic jury, along with the significant costs associated with mounting a defense, can give a defendant manager, and those in his or her organization, many sleepless nights.

EXERCISING POWER

Now, lest you think I am opposed to the use of power, I want to make it clear that I recognize there are times when power must be exercised by the leader.

In our homes, it may be necessary to apply the "board

of education to the seat of learning." At work, there will be times when we need to tell Chucky, "You no longer get to work here."

Certainly, there are legitimate uses of power. Indeed, power is sometimes necessary to meet the legitimate needs of an individual or the organization we are serving. However, whenever I am called upon to exercise power, that is usually a bad day for me as the leader. Why? Because my authority has broken down and I had to resort to my power.

In his inaugural address on the two hundredth anniversary of the presidency in January 1989, new president George Bush offered a prayer about the use of power. "Heavenly Father . . . write on our hearts these words: 'Use power to help people.' For we are given power not to advance our own purposes, nor to make a great show in the world, nor a name. There is but one just use of power, and it is to serve people. Help us to remember it, Lord. Amen."

AUTHORITY AND INFLUENCE

Authority has been defined as the skill of getting others to willingly do your will, because of your personal influence. Having power *over* people is one thing. Having authority *with* people is quite another.

My mother could ask me to do most anything, and I would not think twice about it. Now, let me assure you that my mother has no power—I can run faster than she can now. But Mom has a lot of authority. I would do anything for

Mom. Where did she get her authority from? What supervisor skills seminar did she attend? What new management book has she been reading?

Mom *served*.

My first boss in business, twenty-five years ago, was a tough boss. I still have nightmares of him saying his favorite line to me: "Mediocre, mediocre, mediocre, Jim. That report you submitted was very mediocre."

He would drive me nuts making me constantly redo assignments. Now, deep down, I knew he was right. I got through high school and college doing everything at the last minute. I was just smart enough to get by doing the bare minimum.

But that wasn't good enough for this guy. He was *relentless,* and he often ticked me off. I am sure he was bothered when I complained, pouted, and didn't talk to him for a week, because he was a very nice man who did not enjoy conflict. But he was *more* concerned about me being the best I was capable of becoming.

He was also a great listener and would listen to all of my excuses before telling me what we were going to do; he appreciated me regularly, treated me with respect (like an important person), and was generally very tuned in to my needs.

To this day, this former boss could call me on the telephone for help, 24/7/365, and I would be on the next airplane. My former boss is an old man now and has no power over me. But he has a great deal of authority with me. I would do most anything he needed. Where did he get that authority from? What business book has he been reading?

He *served.*

I didn't like him much for the friction he provided me at the time, but I love him for it now. If it wasn't for his constant prodding and pushing, I would probably still be just getting by, doing the bare minimum. On second thought, by now I probably would not be doing much at all because I was moving in the wrong direction. By now, I would probably be lying on a couch somewhere watching *Days of Our Lives* and eating ice cream and potato chips with a "back condition." He cared too much to allow that to happen.

MORAL AUTHORITY

We have several examples of this distinction between power and authority going on in America today.

When politicians are caught in scandals, particularly sexcapades, the press and pundits will often declare that the person involved has lost his "moral authority." Today we are hearing these words about the Roman Catholic Church — pundits regularly declare that the Church is losing its "moral authority" because of the priest scandal.

Now, what is "moral authority"? That is classic Max Weber–speak, eight decades old.

If a politician caught in sexual shenanigans gave a speech on family values and the importance of marital fidelity, what would be the likely response? It would be all we could do to keep a straight face. Would that speech likely influence anybody listening?

But that is exactly what leadership is. When the leader speaks, people are influenced and become inspired to act.

For the past decade or two in America, I don't think we have been much interested in leadership in Washington, D.C. Good management, yes. When we elect politicians, I think, many of us are interested in people who can manage things well: "Don't mess up the economy; don't foul up my 401(k); try to pass some laws; try to get along with each other; try to stay out of jail."

But are we looking for people to influence us, inspire us to action, and assist us in living successful lives?

In 1964, three out of four people in America said they trusted their government to do the right thing. A recent survey asking the same question showed that 18 percent (less than one in five) trust their government to do the right thing. Influence us? My goodness, we laugh and make jokes about our political leaders. Did you hear about the two elderly women who were walking in an overcrowded cemetery and came upon a grave marked "Here Lies John Smith, a Politician and an Honest Man"? "How awful," said one woman to the other, "that they had to bury two people in the same grave."

Many say, "It's the economy, stupid," and define the success or failure of politicians by how the stock market is doing. Yet, in the year 2000, surveys revealed that more than 90 percent of Americans believed our country was suffering from an erosion of moral and ethical values.

Remember, the ultimate test of leadership is whether people are better off when the leader leaves than when he or she got there. Are the people really being well served by our politicians? Are we getting what we want—great returns on our 401(k) balance—or what we really need, such as a country of character built upon strong moral and ethical values?

Charles de Gaulle, the late French president, once said, "When times are good and people take life easily, people pay lip service to character and keep it at arm's length. But the world clamors for it when danger threatens."

Think of the last fifteen years or so in America. No cold war or world war; good economy; collapse of the Iron Curtain, America becoming the only superpower. Times have been good, and consequently good management has been all we wanted. Since September 11, 2001, things have changed in America. Words like *prayer, country, flag, leadership,* and *patriotism* are popular once again.

The military is well aware that armies do fine with decent management during peacetime. Not so in war. Can you imagine a military leader "managing" his or her troops into battle?

Again, leadership is influence. There was a time in our country when the president spoke from the bully pulpit and people responded. Think of World War II and FDR asking people to sacrifice. And they actually did! That's leadership.

Legitimate authority (influence) must be earned and

does not come from a job title, nameplate, or special perks. If one is going to be in the leadership game for more than a few seasons, he or she had best learn how to build authority with people. Yes, you can get a few seasons out of power, but if you are building your leadership style on power, it will soon become a house of cards, and the symptoms will be coming soon — if they haven't arrived already.

It is important to understand that building influence is not about manipulating, persuading, or pressuring people for *personal* benefit. Leadership is influencing people for *mutual* benefit. Leadership is the willingness to extend oneself and meet the needs of another human being. The choice to seek the greatest good of those one leads is a choice that is freely made and freely given. Leadership is the choice one makes because it is the right thing to do, regardless of the return that may or may not come one's way as a result.

The good news is that authority can be built by most people who have the will to serve others. Stephen Covey, author of *The Seven Habits of Highly Effective People,* put it this way: "Anyone can be a servant-leader. Any one of us can take initiative ourself; it doesn't require that we be appointed a leader, but it does require that we operate from moral authority. The spirit of servant-leadership is the spirit of moral authority."

In a relationship built upon authority, when discipline is required, all the leader may need to do is look the follower in the eye and say, "I am disappointed in you."

In a relationship built upon authority, the follower would probably prefer to be yelled at or written up than to have disappointed the leader. And rest assured: The follower is not going to want to disappoint the leader again any time soon.

That, folks, is the most powerful form of human motivation on the planet.

CHAPTER THREE

On Building Authority

Anyone wanting to be a leader among you
must first be the servant. . . .
If you choose to lead, you must serve.

JESUS CHRIST

IF YOU WERE TO COME INTO MY HOME, YOU WOULD SEE A ton of books neatly arranged on bookshelves. If you were to look more closely, you would find the vast majority of those books to be on the topic of leadership. I have been infatuated with leadership for more than thirty-five years.

Leading with power was a concept I easily grasped and was practicing effectively by the age of two. By the time I reached adolescence, I learned that there were consequences for using power: knuckle sandwiches, extra chores, and broken relationships, to name a few.

I therefore turned my attention to a different type of leadership. The question I became intrigued by was this: How were the great leaders in history able to get people *willingly* to do their will or commit to a cause, even if it meant death? Or more simply put, how did the great leaders of the past get people from "the neck up"?

Knowing from experience and common sense that the use of power is limited in its scope, my quest became "What is the true essence of leadership?"

To answer this question, I have studied great leaders from many fields, including the military, education, religion, politics, business, and athletics, looking for the answer. I have studied mystics and sages from the past and present in my search to uncover the true essence of leadership.

Then one day it dawned on me that I should look at what Jesus had to say about leadership.

THE GREATEST LEADER EVER

Why did I pick Jesus?

For a very pragmatic reason. According to just about any definition of leadership, this man was a great leader. If leadership is about influence, which we know it is, I challenge anyone to name a human being in the history of the world who has had more influence than this one man. Name one who even comes close.

H. G. Wells, the famous author, historian, and atheist, was a harsh critic of Christianity, yet he once remarked, "I am an historian, I am not a believer, but I must confess as an historian that this penniless preacher from Nazareth is irrevocably the very center of history. Jesus Christ is easily the most dominant figure in all history."

Today, one-third of the planet's population, more than 2 billion people, identify themselves as Christians. Eight and a half out of 10 Americans self-identify as Christians. Islam, the next-largest world religion, has half the followers of Christianity. Many countries around the world have national holidays based upon events in Jesus' life. Our calendar measures the passing of time from the days He lived and walked the earth. No intellectually honest person can deny that this solitary life had great influence in history. And He still has it today.

The French general Napoléon Bonaparte put it this way: "Alexander, Caesar, Charlemagne, and I have founded empires. But on what did we rest the creations of our genius? Upon force. Jesus Christ founded his empire upon love, and at this hour, millions would die for him."

THE ESSENCE OF LEADERSHIP

In the book of Matthew in the New Testament, Jesus makes His definitive statement about leadership. The passage has been paraphrased in various ways, but in substance He says that anyone who wishes to be the leader must first be the servant. If you choose to lead, you must serve.

Now, to be completely honest, the first time I read those words I thought it was a nice concept for Sunday at church or for the hereafter but had little relevance to leadership today. After all, we live in a power world, don't we? You have to be in control, in charge, or they will walk all over you. Serve? I have been breaking my back for fifteen years trying to make all of my bosses happy, and now I become the boss, and you tell me I have to serve again? No way!

One of my favorite proverbs teaches, "When the student is ready, the teacher arrives." Not long after I read Jesus' words, I came across Max Weber and came to understand the difference between power and authority. If you cannot grasp the difference between power and authority, you will never understand the point Jesus was trying to make.

Jesus certainly was not talking about leading with power when He said that to lead is to serve. After all, He did not possess traditional power. Caesar, Herod, the Romans, Pilate, and the chief priests — those folks had all the power.

Jesus was talking about leading with authority. In essence, He was saying that if you want to get people to come willingly, if you want to influence people from the neck up, then you must serve. Legitimate leadership, influence, is built upon serving, sacrificing, and seeking the greatest good of those being led. Influence does not come because of a title or an army. Influence must be earned. There are no shortcuts.

In my previous work, I detail several examples of great world leaders who had no power but operated from a position of authority and accomplished things that changed the world. Leaders like Mahatma Gandhi, Martin Luther King Jr., Nelson Mandela, and Mother Teresa.

I want to say it again: Influence, legitimate leadership, is built upon service and sacrifice. Talking about serving and sacrificing to business audiences these days can be a stretch when there are many employees who define "sacrifice" as having to pay $10 a month more for their health-insurance benefits!

To further illustrate this point, I was watching the Super Bowl recently and observed a $9 million per year athlete on the sidelines holding up a handwritten sign that read, "I ♥ MOM," while yelling at the top of his lungs, "Hi, Mom; hi, Mom!"

What is up with that?

Perhaps you know the old saying that the best way to get a brawl going in the local tavern is simply by making a derogatory comment about somebody's mother. That will usually get the chairs and tables flying!

What is up with that?

I will tell you what is up with that.

Mom has served.

THE LAW OF THE HARVEST

Folks, this is not rocket science.

I have taught these principles to school-age children, and they easily grasp the concept. It is simply the "Law of the Harvest"—that is, you reap what you sow. You sow service and sacrifice; you extend yourselves for others and seek their greatest good; you will build influence with them. As the cliché goes, "You go to the wall for me, and I'll go to the wall for you."

Suppose you have a sixty-foot tree in your backyard that has been dead so long that it has lost its bark and has turned gray. You would like to have it professionally removed but cannot afford the serious expense involved.

One Saturday morning, your neighbor, the one who kind of bugs you, shows up with his chainsaw and says, "Let's take that bad boy down. You and me. Now."

He spends the entire weekend with you sawing, cutting, chopping, stacking, and raking. He even helps you dig out the stump. Now, it is Sunday night and you are in your garage with him, kicking back and sipping a soda. How do you feel about your neighbor now?

I don't know about you, but every time I drive by my neighbor's house, I will be looking at his yard, trying to figure a way to help him out. I will *actively* seek out opportunities to be of service to him. Again, this is not quantum mechanics. You serve me, I'll serve you.

BEWARE THE 10 PERCENT

For the life of me, I cannot understand why more leaders cannot grasp the simple truth that if you get your people what they need, they will get you everything you need. Our leadership will be defined not by what we accomplish but by what we get accomplished through others. If we get people what they need, they will make us look great!

Do you believe this? Do you believe in the law of the harvest? Do you believe that we really do reap what we sow?

Perhaps you are skeptical because you know that people sometimes will not respond to authority—and this is true. In my seminars, I tell audiences that predictably, 10 percent or so of the people you lead will not only not respond to your authority but will try to sabotage you and everything you are trying to build. There are some bad folks out there. If you had any illusions about that, I hope September 11, 2001, shattered them.

Please be careful of becoming a skeptic and cynic because of the few bad apples out there. I have known many, many managers who have been beaten down by the 10 percent and begin painting everyone with the same broad brush: "You can't trust anyone anymore," or "People are no longer motivated," or "People won't work hard for a living," or "These young kids don't know what loyalty is." What a shame that most organizations draft interminable policies, procedures, and handbooks for the 10 percent of the folks who probably shouldn't be there anyway.

My advice to my audiences is if they have any of that 10 percent in the group they lead, get them out as soon as possible. As one of my favorite CEOs, who also happens to be a servant leader, likes to say when he fires one of these, "I love you, and I'll miss you."

Even in your home, if your son takes the family car and credit cards every Friday night without permission, there comes a point in time when you have to say, "You no longer get to live here, son."

That is known as tough love, and my experience is that it is *not* exercised nearly enough in the vast majority of organizations today.

I'M NOT MOTHER TERESA

One of the dangers of giving historical and sometimes dramatic examples of great leaders of authority is that people can quickly come to the conclusion (excuse?) that obviously they can never aspire to that level of greatness, so what's the point of even trying?

In my seminars, when I mention these great leaders from the past, I sometimes get outbursts like "What am I supposed to do, die for my people like Jesus? Go on a hunger fast like Gandhi? Find some lepers in our cafeteria to help like Mother Teresa? I'm just a supervisor at Sears, for goodness' sake. Give me a break!"

My response usually goes something like this.

"I use dramatic examples from history to get people's attention. The good news is that anytime we extend ourselves, sacrifice, and serve others, we build authority and thereby influence. Nobody is asking anyone to die at the office or even to give blood to the Red Cross. But how about extending ourselves to appreciate our people? What about treating them like important people? Perhaps we could sacrifice by taking a little more time to listen to them. How about working on being more trusting and less controlling? Maybe we could lend a hand and assist people to be the best they are capable of becoming. Can we give that much at the office?"

ANYONE CAN SERVE

Martin Luther King Jr. recognized this truth: "Everybody can be great because anybody can serve. You don't have to have a college degree to serve. You don't have to make your subject and verb agree to serve. . . . You don't have to know the second theory of thermodynamics in physics to serve. You only need a heart full of grace. A soul generated by love."

Serving and sacrificing for others can be accomplished in many, many ways. When we are dedicated to identifying and meeting the legitimate needs of others (serving), we will often be put into the position of having to make sacrifices. We may have to sacrifice our ego, our lust for power, our pride, and other self-interests for the greater good. We may have to sacrifice our need to be liked, our bad habit of avoiding conflict, our desire to have all of the answers, to look good, to always be right. When we serve others, we will have to forgive, apologize, and give others credit even when we do not feel like it. When we extend ourselves for others, we will be rejected, underappreciated, and even taken advantage of at times. Indeed, we will have to sacrifice and subordinate anything that gets in the way of doing the right thing with and for people.

Unfortunately, many in leadership positions find this too high a price to pay. Many believe that once they have arrived as the leader, it is *their* turn to be served. Says Peter Drucker, "No leader is worth his salt who won't set up chairs."

The good news is that anyone can serve others. Each of us has the capacity to make a difference in another person's life, and this is especially true for those of us in leadership positions.

Anne Frank, who died in one of Hitler's death camps, stated this point eloquently when she said, "How wonderful it is that nobody need wait a single moment before starting to improve the world."

EMOTIONAL TWO-YEAR-OLDS

If you want to understand what the basic nature of human beings looks like, just observe two-year-olds in action. Their character can be summed up in two words: "Me first!"

This basic nature of humankind is cute in a two-year-old but rather ugly in a fifty-year-old.

I have spent a career dealing with many executives and managers who have never successfully gotten over their "terrible twos." Behind all the nice trappings — charm, wit, intelligence, and an Armani suit — is a two-year-old stating, "Me first; the heck with you!"

My wife, in her counseling practice, often deals with emotional two-year-olds. People come through her door, wallowing in *me*. "My needs, my wants, my desires, my issues, my inner child — me, me, me!" People totally consumed with *me*. My wife will tell you that these people are some of the most unhappy and miserable souls she has ever known. It is another one of those strange and beautiful paradoxes of life that when we break out of "me" and extend ourselves for others and meet their legitimate needs, our needs will also be met.

If we desire to become effective leaders and human

beings, we *must* get over that "me first" problem. We must grow up. When we sign up to be the leader, other people's needs become primary. To this day in the U.S. military, the troops eat first, officers last.

Phil Jackson is a famous basketball coach known for getting superstars and difficult personalities to work together to win championships. In his book *Sacred Hoops: Spiritual Lessons of a Hardwood Warrior,* he writes, "The most effective way to forge a winning team is to call on the players' need to connect with something larger than themselves. Even for those who don't consider themselves 'spiritual' in a conventional sense, creating a successful team—whether it's an NBA champion or a record-setting sales force—is essentially a spiritual act. It requires the individuals involved to surrender their self-interest for the greater good so that the whole adds up to more than the sum of its parts."

Some have said to me over the years, "Well, I'm just not into all that serving-and-sacrificing jazz. I've got to look out for numero uno, because if I don't no one else will."

If you are stuck in the "me first" mode, that is a choice. If so, please don't make another choice—of signing up to be a leader. Please don't have children if you are into that "me first" mind-set. Please don't get married and have someone entrust his or her life to you. Please don't make employees spend 50 percent of their waking hours working for someone with a "me first" or a "my career" agenda.

Make a different choice! Take a solo sailboat trip around the world and write often. As poet W. H. Auden once quipped, "We're here on earth to do good for others. What the others are here for, I don't know."

THE JOY IN SERVING

As noted earlier, when we serve others and seek their greatest good, it will often become necessary to extend ourselves and sacrifice. It is difficult work and not for the faint of heart.

If you study great leaders of authority from the past like Jesus, Gandhi, and Mother Teresa, you often find them speaking about the great joy they derive from serving others.

The late, great American psychiatrist and author Karl Menninger lived to be nearly a hundred years old. Before he died in 1990, he was asked what he would recommend to a person about to suffer a nervous breakdown. He replied, "Lock up your house, go across the railroad tracks, find someone in need, and do something for them."

Go get out of "me" for a while, and "me" will start doing a lot better.

I once watched *Larry King Live,* when his guests were Christopher Reeve and his lovely wife, Dana. As you probably know, Reeve broke his neck in a freak horseback-riding accident and has been paralyzed from the neck down for many years. I cannot imagine what this couple has been through and continues to endure.

Here is part of the dialogue that evening.

LARRY KING: Aren't there days when you get down?

DANA REEVE: When we're feeling sorry for ourselves, the first thing we try to do is reach out to help someone else. And it's amazing how you can start feeling better because of that.

CHRISTOPHER REEVE: Take action. Get the attention off yourself. That's number one.

Abraham Lincoln, in his simple, concise way, said, "When I do good, I feel good."

So we're back to choices again. We must decide if we will choose to serve others or merely serve ourselves.

In the end, we must choose between being a servant leader and a self-serving leader.

CHAPTER FOUR

On Leadership and Love

What's love got to do with it?
Tina Turner

DEATH AND CHOICES, RIGHT?

I made a choice over a dozen years ago to introduce the concept of "love" into my business seminars.

Now, where I come from (Detroit), that's a pretty big risk, especially with my male audiences! They can be right with me, even cheering me on, until I get to love. Then their eyes begin to glaze over, their chins drop to their chests, and they nervously begin kicking the carpet.

Yet as I have studied the great leaders of authority, from Jesus to Martin Luther King Jr., from Gandhi to Mother Teresa, from Herb Kelleher to Jack Welch, I am struck by how these leaders constantly talk and write about that little four-letter word: *love*.

Geoffey Colvin of *Fortune* wrote a very special article in November 2001 entitled "What's Love Got to Do with It?"

in which he talked about Southwest's Kelleher and GE's Welch and their fanatical use of the word *love*. (You can find the article at http://www.jameshunter.com.)

I'm convinced that the discomfort many feel around the word *love,* particularly in business settings, is because we are thinking about love as a feeling. The English language has butchered the word because we almost always associate love with positive feelings, with the exception of when we are playing tennis.

For example, I can love my job, my dog, my home, my wife, and my '68 Camaro. As long as I "feel good" about something, I can say I love it. If we do not feel good about something, we probably would not associate the word *love* with it.

LOVE THE VERB

Vince Lombardi, the legendary football coach, once commented, "I don't necessarily have to *like* my associates, but as a man I must *love* them."

Love? Now, wait a minute—wasn't Lombardi the tough guy who loved to say, "Winning isn't everything, it's the only thing!"? Many are unaware that Lombardi tried very hard to distance himself from that quote later in life, saying, "I wish to h— I'd never said the d— thing. . . . I meant the effort . . . having a goal. . . . I sure as h— didn't mean for people to crush human values and morality." Lombardi clearly understood the distinction between the love of feeling (emotion) and the love of the will (volition).

Emotional love, with its passion, romance, and warm fuzzies, is the language of love, the fruit of love, the expression of love. But it is not what love *is*.

Volitional love is the love of the will. Volitional love is the choice, the willingness of a person to be attentive to the legitimate needs, best interests, and welfare of another, regardless of how he or she happens to feel on certain days.

One of my favorite authors is the late Englishman, professor, author, and Christian apologist C. S. Lewis. Lewis wrote that love "does not mean an emotion. It is a state not of the feelings but of the will; that state of the will which we have naturally about ourselves, and must learn to have about other people. . . . It means that we wish [seek] our own good."

Remember, any scum of the earth can love people they like. Hitler, Stalin, and Saddam Hussein were wonderful to the people they liked and to the people who could do something for them. Anyone can kiss up to important people. But loving people we do not like?

This is the type of love Vince Lombardi was talking about. Lombardi once said that he and his players might not like each other at times, but he was committed to demanding excellence and pushing his players to be the best they could be. *That* is how much he cared. He said his love would be *relentless*.

You may find this difficult to believe, but there are times my wife does not like me very much. But that fact has nothing to do with whether she continues to love me. Her feelings have nothing to do with the choice she makes to remain kind, respectful, forgiving, and committed — all of the things love *is* even though old Jimbo is acting like a jerk this week. Are you with me?

As mentioned earlier, *love* is a word used frequently at Southwest Airlines. In fact, the company's advertising jingle for many years was "The airline that love built." Southwest's people not only talk about love — they work hard to behave with love. Herb Kelleher, Southwest's founder, said, "A company is stronger if it is bound by love rather than by fear."

I will be using the word *love* quite a bit in this book, so I want you to be clear what I am talking about when I use it. I am certainly not talking about how we feel about people or suggesting we violate sexual-harassment laws. I am talking about how we *behave* every day. Are we interested in helping people grow and become the best they can be? Are we extending ourselves for others even when we may not feel like it? Are we seeking the greatest good of those we lead?

For the purposes of this book, love will be defined as:

The act(s) of extending yourself for others by identifying and meeting their legitimate needs and seeking their greatest good.

The proper paraphrase of love is "Love is as love does."

DON'T TELL ME—SHOW ME

Nearly eight hundred years ago, Saint Francis of Assisi is said to have exhorted his followers to "preach the Gospel at all times, but only use words if necessary."

I can remember in my younger and wilder days running around with friends carousing in bars and other places I probably shouldn't have been. It would strike me rather odd when my married buddy would say at three o'clock in the morning, "I better get home to my wife. I sure love that gal." I can remember thinking, "You love her and you're out until all hours doing this stuff?"

Another disconnect to me was when a buddy with children would tell me how much he loved his kids but couldn't carve out an hour a week to be with them. He would lecture me incessantly about the importance of the *quality* of time, not the *quantity* of time. I remember wondering, is love as love says, or is love as love does?

Back in the "dark" years of my consulting work, when I was fighting unions and working with some very dysfunctional organizations, I used to place bets with my partner on how long it would take before we heard the "asset speech" from the CEO.

You know how that speech goes: "Jim, before we get started, you need to know something very important. You need to know that our employees are our greatest asset. We love our people here."

Whenever I was on the receiving end of the asset

speech, I felt like blurting out: Oh, is that so? May I speak to Chucky on the forklift and see if that's true? We will be able to diagnose this in about thirty seconds. (By the way, the line should *not* be "employees are our greatest asset" but rather "the *right* employees are our greatest asset.")

People are alike in that they will generally say the right things. But I must confess that as I get older, I am much more impressed with what people *do* than with what they *say*.

Ralph Waldo Emerson put it succinctly when he said, "What you are shouts so loudly in my ears I cannot hear what you say."

THE QUALITIES OF LOVE AND LEADERSHIP

My seminar and workshop participants over the years have covered the full spectrum, from press operators to school-children, from sanitation workers to physicians, from Boy Scouts to Fortune 500 directors.

Often in my seminars, I would ask participants to list for me the qualities of a great leader. I was interested in knowing the collective wisdom of a large group around what mattered most when it came to leadership.

I was initially surprised to find the "Leadership Quali-ties" lists to be virtually the same from one group to the next. The common responses would include being honest, respectful, firm but fair; appreciative; having good commu-nication skills; being committed; and being predictable.

During this same time period, I attended the wedding of a close friend. Just before the couple recited their wedding vows, the pastor read the famous passage that is spoken at nearly every Christian wedding: 1 Corinthians 13, better known as the "Love Passage."

Now, I had heard these words spoken a hundred times before and even had them read at my own wedding. But for some reason, I heard the words differently this time. Perhaps the student was finally ready.

This is what the pastor said:

Love is *patient,* love is *kind,* it is not puffed up or arrogant *(humble)*, it does not act unbecomingly *(respectful)*, it does not seek its own *(selfless)*, it does not take into account a wrong suffered *(forgiving)*, it does not rejoice in unrighteousness but rejoices in the truth *(honest)*, it bears all things, endures all things, it never fails *(committed)*.

The list he read to the charming couple was virtually the same list I was hearing in my leadership seminars! Here was a two-thousand-year-old definition of love and leadership as relevant and applicable today as ever. I remember thinking at the time that perhaps there really was nothing new under the sun.

Now where on that list do you see any feelings? Where is the part about "love is romance, love is passion, love is flowers and candy" in that definition? I don't know about you, but I see a lot of *work* on that list. I think that is why that list is read so often at weddings — once the feelings pass for a season it's time to get to work. As Tony Campolo, the well-known professor, author, and speaker, has said, "At every wedding we have an opportunity for a marriage. But we never really know what we've got until the feelings pass for a time. Then we see."

Anyone can do courtship and honeymoon. Anybody can talk about love. I think it was Zsa Zsa Gabor who once said, "Twenty men in one year, piece of cake, darlink. One man for twenty years, that's a real problem."

The same is true with leadership. Anyone can sign up to be a spouse, parent, boss, coach, or teacher, but when the going gets tough, then we see what we've got.

What I have come to believe about these eight qualities of love is that not only are they a splendid definition of love, they also epitomize the very essence of leadership. And not only do these qualities define leadership — they embody the true meaning of *character*. In fact, these are the same qualities we've been teaching our little eight-year-old for seven years now. Over and over and over again. More about the work of building character later.

Loving others is about doing the right thing. Leadership is about doing the right thing. Character is about doing the right thing. Again, leadership development and character development are *one*.

THE ESSENTIALS DEFINED

After that wedding many years ago, I could not wait to get home and compare that two-thousand-year-old definition to the "Leadership Qualities" lists from my seminars to confirm the near-perfect match. This compelled me to open my dictionary to better define these behaviors.

Leadership Requires Patience

The definition of patience is to "show self-control."

Is this quality of character important for a leader? Not only is it important—it is essential, because patience and self-control are the essential building blocks of character, and hence leadership.

I believe self-control is better described using the phrase "impulse control." We are teaching impulse control to our little girl every day by coaching her to respond not according to what she "feels" like doing but according to what is the right thing to do.

Without control over our basic desires, whims, appetites, and other urges, we have little hope of behaving with character in difficult situations. A habit must be developed by responding from principles rather than urges in order for us to be effective leaders. In short, we must get our impulses under control. We must get the head (values) in charge of the heart (emotions).

Patience and self-control are essential to healthy relationships. If you doubt this, then ask yourself this question: Do you have good relationships with people who are out of control?

Patience and self-control are both about being consistent and predictable in mood and actions. Are you a safe person? Easy to be with? Approachable? Can you handle contrary opinion? Criticism?

Now, I am not suggesting that we cannot be passionate in what we do or that we have no emotions. Passion (commitment) is an essential leadership quality that we will discuss later. We can be very passionate in what we do while maintaining our patience and self-control with people. If you are not a safe person for people to readily approach with the bad news as well as the good, look out.

I often get people in my seminars who readily admit to having bad tempers and will even admit that they sometimes rage at people and have inappropriate outbursts. They are usually quick to defend their behavior by saying things like "That's just the way I am," or "As you can see, I'm a redhead," or "I'm just like my father was."

When I hear this, I usually respond by saying, "So when was the last time you 'lost it' and had a fit with the CEO of the company? How about with a valued customer?"

Of course, they answer, "Why, never!"

To which I respond, "Isn't it interesting that you can control yourself with the CEO or a customer but not with the people working for you? Why do you think that is?"

I know of a guy who played adult-league softball for many years after high school. He was a great guy, but unfortunately for the umpires he had a temper that was the joke of the league. If a questionable call was made, he immediately would be yelling and spraying saliva all over the poor ump, usually resulting in ejection from the game.

One year, the league hired a new umpire who just happened to be the pastor at a local church. You guessed it. It happened to be the difficult player's pastor. Now, how many games do you think he was thrown out of that year? You guessed it again. Zero.

When asked how he achieved the feat of going a whole season without getting kicked out of a single game, his response was simply "Heck, you can't yell at the pastor."

Now, you tell me: Are patience and self-control choices?

Anger is a natural and healthy emotion, and passion is a wonderful quality to possess, as we will see later. However, acting out on anger or passion and violating the rights of others is inappropriate and damages relationships. This is the part that can and must be controlled.

Leadership Requires Kindness

The dictionary definition of kindness is "to give attention, appreciation, and encouragement to people." The second definition listed is "to display common courtesy to others."

Kindness is an act of love (verb) because it requires us to reach out to others, to extend ourselves, even to people we may not be particularly fond of. Kindness and common courtesy are about doing the things that help relationships flow smoothly. This includes extending ourselves for others by appreciating them, encouraging them, being courteous, listening well, and giving credit and praise for efforts made.

William James, the great American philosopher and psychologist, taught that human beings at the core of their personality have the *need* to be appreciated.

Have you been appreciating your kids lately? Your

spouse? Your boss? Your employees, who spend one-half of their waking hours giving efforts under your leadership? Your teammates? Mother Teresa often said that people crave appreciation more than they crave bread.

Effective leaders encourage those around them to be the best they can be. Effective leaders push, cajole, pull, and encourage others to raise their level of play. They encourage others by their willingness to share their knowledge and experiences and are a constant, positive influence to the people around them. Remember, you don't have to be the boss to encourage and influence others.

Common courtesy is doing the little things that make a house a home. Little things like saying please; thank you; I'm sorry, I was wrong. Little things like being the first one to say, "Good morning," in the hallway.

Kindness is the WD-40 of human relationships.

Leadership Requires Humility

My dictionary defines humility as "displaying an absence of pride, arrogance, or pretense; behaving authentically."

Humility, like *love,* is another word that has been butchered in the English language. The opposite of humility is arrogance, boastfulness, or pride. Many people therefore mistakenly associate being humble with being passive, overly modest, self-effacing, or even a "poor pitiful me" type.

To the contrary, humble leaders are not afflicted with some unbalanced sense of their inferiority. Humble leaders can be as bold as a lion when it comes to their sense of values, morality, and doing the right thing. They can be as fierce as a pit bull when it comes to staying focused and on mission, hitting margin targets, and holding people accountable.

Humble leaders are simply those who have stopped fooling themselves about who they really are. Humble leaders know that they put their pants on the same way as everyone else. They know that they are only a disaster or two away from the bottom of the pile. They know that they came into the world with nothing and will leave with nothing (you will never see a funeral hearse pulling a U-Haul). Humble leaders have gotten over themselves and their terrible twos. Humble leaders have grown up.

Humble leaders display a willingness, even an eagerness, to listen to the opinions of others and are wide open to contrary opinion. Humble leaders know they do not have to have all of the answers, and they are perfectly okay with that. English critic John Ruskin observed, "Really great men have a curious feeling that the greatness is not in them, but through them. Therefore, they are humble."

Humble leaders do not take themselves or events too seriously. Humble leaders are able to laugh at themselves and the world, which is so important because people have a need to have fun. Humble leaders are quick to give credit to others and do not seek out credit and adulation for themselves; they are secure in who and what they are.

I have met many, many people in leadership positions who seem incapable of saying things like "I don't know," or "What do you think?" or "Challenge my thinking," or "I am sorry, I was wrong," or "You did that much better than I could have." After getting to know these people, I generally find that they are insecure and uncomfortable in their own skins.

In *Good to Great*, Jim Collins refers to the highest performing level of leadership, what he labels "Level 5," and says, "Level 5 leaders embody a paradoxical mix of personal humility and professional will. They are ambitious, to be sure, but ambitious first and foremost for the company, not themselves."

Humble leaders view their leadership as an awesome responsibility. They view leadership as a position of trust and stewardship and take having people entrusted to their care very seriously. They are not focused on their "management rights," nor do they lay awake at night worrying about office politics and who will get the corner office. Rather, they are focused on their leadership *responsibilities* and often lay awake at night thinking about whether they are effectively meeting the needs of their people.

Humble leaders are authentic. They do not walk around wearing "I've got it all together" masks. Humble leaders are willing to be open and vulnerable because they have their egos under control and do not operate from delusions of grandeur, believing they are indispensable to their organizations. They are well aware that cemeteries are full of indispensable people.

Humble leaders are secure in knowing they have strengths and limitations, knowing full well that there are many others who could do the job as well or better than they could. Humble leaders know they are capable of making errors and are conscious that the greatest fault of all is believing you have none.

A wise mystic centuries ago commented, "If we could truly see ourselves for what we really are, we would be very humble indeed."

Dust to dust, ashes to ashes. I once heard a pastor at a funeral say, "Nobody is getting out of this thing alive."

Humble leaders are able to keep things in perspective.

Leadership Requires Respect

My dictionary defines respect as "treating people like they are important."

The people around the leader know full well that he or she is capable of respecting others, as they see him or her do it every time someone important comes around. But what about the little people or the challenging ones? Do they get that same respect?

Ethel Waters, the well-known black singer and actress of the 1920s, was fond of saying, "God don't create no junk. He just creates people with behavior problems."

So true. And guess what? You and I have some of those behavior problems, too. I tell people in my seminars, "If you don't think you have any behavior problems that you can work on and improve, put arrogance at the top of your list. And if you still think you have no issues to work on, stand up now and we'll have the people on your team point them out to you!"

An effective way that leaders can give respect and build trust is by developing the skill of delegating responsibilities to others so they can grow and develop. Proper delegating communicates respect for another person's skills and abilities. Delegating responsibilities is a wonderful way to demonstrate trust, which, of course, is a two-way street. If we desire trust from others, we must give trust to them. The discretion and independent judgment we want our people to possess only come by exercising discretion and independent judgment.

I once had a seminar participant say to me, "My daddy taught me respect is earned. Therefore, I respect only people who have earned my respect!"

"Your daddy lied" was my response.

Respect isn't *earned* when you are the leader—respect is *given* when you are the leader. Don't people get respect for being human? Don't people get respect for working for the same organization that you do? In fact, if I was a shareholder, I could argue that the leader's job is to help his or her people win and be successful. The leader will respect them when they earn it? And when might that be?

Recall the definition of love. Love is a choice, the willingness to extend oneself for others and seek their greatest good *regardless* of whether they have earned it or have got it coming. Love (leadership) does not pause to create an Excel spreadsheet, putting people's pluses and minuses in columns before hitting the autosum button to determine if respect is due. Rather, the leader gives respect. The leader *chooses* to treat all people like important people, even when they behave poorly or "don't deserve it."

Effective leaders understand that everyone is important and adds value to an organization. And if they do not add value to the organization, whose fault is that? Why are they still there? Again, everyone is important. The only difference is that people have different job responsibilities and the market compensates those responsibilities differently.

Put another way, think of servant leadership as *primus inter pares,* translated as "first among equals." Again, Herb Kelleher of Southwest Airlines: "My mother taught me . . . that positions and titles mean absolutely nothing. They're just adornments; they don't represent the substance of anybody. . . . She taught me that every person and every job is worth as much as any other person and any other job."

Leadership Requires Selflessness

Selflessness is defined as "meeting the needs of others." What a beautiful definition of leadership: to meet the needs of others.

During seminars, I am often asked, "Even before my own needs?" to which I respond, "Even before your own needs, grasshopper."

When you signed up to be the leader, that's what you signed up to do.

The will to serve and sacrifice for others, the willingness

to set aside our wants and needs in seeking the greatest good for others — this is what it means to be selfless. This is what it means to be the leader.

I often get challenged about serving others by indignant people who will say, "Yeah, that serving stuff sounds great, but you don't know my boss!" or "You don't know my spouse," or "You don't know the kind of employees I am dealing with!"

I generally respond by saying they must work to kick out that "stinkin' thinkin' " because they are already on the wrong track! The road to servant leadership lies not in trying to fix or change others but in working on changing and improving ourselves. Russian novelist Leo Tolstoy once remarked, "Everyone wants to change the world, but no one wants to change himself."

How true! Our world changes when we change. Besides that, we do not have the power to change other people. As Alcoholics Anonymous wisely teaches, the only person you can change is yourself. If each of us cleared the trash from our own yard, we would soon have a clean street.

Service and sacrifice were more thoroughly discussed in chapter 3, so rather than be redundant, we will move on.

Leadership Requires Forgiveness

My dictionary defines forgiveness as "letting go of resentment."

People often remark that they believe forgiveness to be a strange character skill to have on a leadership list, yet I remain convinced it is one of the most important.

Why?

Because when you are the leader, people are going to make mistakes. A lot of them. Your boss, your peers, your subordinates, your spouse, your kids, your teammates are going to screw up, make mistakes, and let you down. People will hurt you, sometimes deeply. Many will not make the efforts you believe they should or care as deeply as you do. Some will fail to respond to all the effort you have put in. A few will try to take advantage of you.

Which is why it is essential for the leader to develop the skill (habit) of accepting limitations in others and the capacity to tolerate imperfection. The leader must develop the skill of letting go of the resentment that often lingers when people hurt us or let us down. After all, anyone could lead perfect people, if only there were any.

Letting go of resentment is not about being passive, a doormat for the world. Letting go is not about letting people get away with bad behavior or pretending the bad behavior is acceptable. To do those things would not be behaving with integrity.

Rather, forgiveness involves going to people and communicating assertively how what they have done has affected you, dealing with it, and then letting go of any lingering resentment. Buddy Hackett put it well: "While you're carrying a grudge, they're out dancing!"

This wonderful quality of character can be developed over time with practice and courage. It can be a difficult skill to develop because when our pride and feelings are hurt, we give ourselves many justifications for not letting people off the hook. It takes a secure, mature individual to develop this skill. As Gandhi once observed, "The weak can never forgive. Forgiveness is the attribute of the strong."

I have known many managers who have ruined their careers because their feelings and pride got in the way and they could not forgive others and let go of their resentment.

Any decent psychologist will tell you that resentment destroys the human personality. People who harbor resentment, who seek revenge and obsess about what others have done to them, get consumed and often become hateful and spiteful human beings. Author Hermann Hesse, whose writings inspired Robert Greenleaf, once wrote, "Whenever we hate someone, it is because we hate some part of ourselves in his image. We don't get excited about anything that is not in ourselves."

Some may say, "That's easy for you to say. But what if a drunk driver killed your child? What if a maniac murdered your wife? What if your sales guy blew the biggest deal of the year because of something stupid? Would you be so quick to forgive?"

I wonder myself. But that seems to me a bit like trying to do advanced trigonometry before having learned addition and subtraction. Perhaps we should begin practicing and developing this character habit with the people around us every day rather than worrying about forgiving serial killers.

What about practicing with people who have committed lesser atrocities? Perhaps we could forgive a coworker for talking down to us. Or forgive a neighbor who behaved poorly one Sunday afternoon. Or let a boss off the hook because he or she embarrassed you in a moment of anger last year. Or cut a family member some slack after holding a grudge for thirty years.

SEPARATING PEOPLE FROM BEHAVIOR

If you have ever taken a human-resources course on constructive discipline, you've probably heard the instructor make statements that sound silly and nonsensical on the surface. Comments like "When you discipline an employee, you must separate the person from his or her behavior."

Usually someone in the audience will respond, "Separate the person from his behavior? How stupid is that? He's the jerk who did it—fire him!"

Of course, what the instructor means is that we all do bad things but aren't necessarily bad people. For example, you should not say to an employee, "You're stupid!" Exactly how is an employee supposed to fix that? Do you have some IQ pills in the first-aid box?

Rather, you should say, "The report you submitted does not meet our standards here." Now, *that* is something the employee can do something about.

You don't say to an employee, "You're lazy!" Rather, "You have been tardy four times this month." *That* is something the employee can do something about.

Theologians often refer to this as "separating the sin from the sinner," which I must admit I once believed to be a rather silly distinction.

Silly until I realized there was one person on the planet with whom I do that routinely.

THE BIGGEST JERK I KNOW

There is this one guy I know who commits the most ridiculous blunders and absurdities you can imagine. You would not believe the foolish things this guy does that hurt me personally, affecting my business and even my family. Yet I am usually quick to get over it and overlook the brainless things he does. I am generally quick to conclude that those were just some things he *did,* but it is not the person he *is.* I mean, he really is a good guy.

And just who is this nincompoop?

You guessed it. Me!

Think about how quick we are to look beyond our own bad behavior. Think how effortless it is to separate our behavior from ourselves. Are we as willing to let others off the hook as easily as we do ourselves?

Forgiveness is an attribute of love, so the question now becomes, are we willing to love others as we love ourselves? Remember, we are talking about love the *verb,* not how we *feel* about ourselves. Indeed, there are times when I don't like my own company, but I still continue to look out for number one. Love is looking out for others and seeking their greatest good, like we do for ourselves.

There are other payoffs to developing this quality of character (skill) of forgiveness. As I write this today, a front-page headline in *USA Today* reads, "What Makes People Happy." The article discusses recently published research about what drives happiness in people. According to University of Michigan psychologist Christopher Peterson, forgiveness is the trait most strongly linked to happiness. "It's the queen of all virtues, and probably the hardest to come by," he reports.

Leadership Requires Honesty

My dictionary defines honesty as "being free from deception."

Few would disagree that honesty and integrity are essential qualities of character that a leader must possess. Surveys have shown for decades that these are the qualities of character people most want in their leader.

If you do not believe that these qualities are essential to leadership, just ask yourself this question: Do you have good relationships with people you do not trust? Are those the people who inspire you?

Trust is the glue that holds relationships together. If my wife and I do not have fundamental trust in our relationship, it would be difficult if not impossible for our organization (marriage) to survive. Without trust, an organization is a house of cards without the glue. How does one build trust? By being trustworthy, of course. Behaving with honesty and integrity builds trust.

I have been in many, many organizations whose executives talk about trust but whose actions betray what they truly believe. Their true beliefs are visible in the form of time clocks, secret meetings, volumes of working rules, special keys to certain doors only for special people, nondisclosure of financial information (including salary information), and on and on.

Organizations often talk about being like a "family" and then fire or lay off people in the late afternoon so as to avoid a "scene." Then comes a deafening silence for days following the event. One of our "greatest assets" just disappears, and nothing is said! How dysfunctional would you consider a family to be if people just started disappearing from the dinner table and nothing was said except for the occasional "Daddy and Johnny mutually agreed that Johnny should leave"?

A major aspect of honesty and being free from deception is in how we hold people accountable for their actions. If we fail to do so, we are not leading honestly, because accountability is our responsibility as leaders, along with helping people be the best they can be. It is deceptive behavior because failure to hold people accountable creates an illusion that everything is okay, and everything is *not* okay. We will spend much of the next chapter discussing accountability and its fundamental importance to leadership.

Another form of honesty, one that organizations do not talk nearly enough about, is being free from duplicitous behavior like gossip, backstabbing, and pairing. I see these behaviors running rampant in institutions all over America. It's as if people get a job and now they have license to backstab and character-assassinate others at will. Is this honest behavior?

Pairing is a destructive alliance between two or more people. These are people who like to break off and talk about the group rather than bringing issues to the group so they can be dealt with. This behavior is hugely destructive to the team and is dishonest.

I tell people that if they are engaged in duplicitous behavior as described above, it is like eating double cheeseburgers and drinking triple chocolate malts on their character diet. They are damaging their character, and everyone is watching.

COMMUNICATION AND TRUST

Building trust requires effort.

Empathic listening is one of the most effective ways I know to build trust, and this skill will be discussed in more detail in the next chapter. Another way we build or damage trust is by how we verbally communicate. The four common ways people communicate are aggressive, passive, passive-aggressive, and assertive.

Aggressive people are generally open and direct but often violate people's rights in the process. You can identify these people by the trail of bodies they leave in their wake. Passive people are those who serve as the doormats for the world and allow people to take advantage of them. Both of these styles damage trust because it is difficult, perhaps impossible, to build trust without treating people with respect and dignity. Neither of these styles communicates respect for the receiver.

By far the most common form of communication I observe in organizations is passive-aggressive. This type of indirect communication comes in the form of sarcasm, the silent treatment, mind games, political games, secret agendas, and other manipulations that damage trust. Passive-aggressive communication is indirect in its nature but fully intends to send a message. This manipulative and indirect approach is hugely destructive to establishing and building relationships.

The proper communication skill that serves effective leaders well is the skill of assertiveness. Now, assertiveness looks just like aggressive behavior in that it is open, honest, and direct. The difference is that assertive people do not violate people's rights in the process. Assertive people are willing to tell the truth whether that truth is good news or bad news; their behavior is open and direct yet respectful.

I have known many leaders who shy away from delivering bad news to their people about their performance or organizational issues such as cutbacks or layoffs. Guess what? Your people can take it! They've dealt with much tougher issues in their everyday lives.

Delivering bad news in an up-front, straightforward, and honest way is a perfect opportunity to develop trust and credibility with people. This direct approach shows you can be trusted because you shoot straight and do not shy away from the truth, whatever it is. This is what integrity is about.

Integrity comes from the same root word as the mathematical term *integer,* which means a *whole* number. Think of integrity as being *wholly* congruent and aligned in thoughts, words, and actions. Integrity is behaving out of right values consistently and predictably, both in public as well as in private. As Gandhi put it, "One man cannot do right in one department of life whilst he is occupied in doing wrong in any other department. Life is one indivisible whole."

Leadership Requires Commitment

My dictionary defines commitment as "sticking to your choice."

I believe that commitment is perhaps the most important character quality a leader can possess. I say this because behaving consistently with the character qualities described in this chapter will be accomplished only through a strong will and solid commitment.

I have found the best servant leaders to be very committed people in whatever they have chosen to do. Servant leadership requires commitment and passion for personal and organizational continuous improvement. It requires a passion for doing what you say you are going to do, following through on promises, and finishing what is started. It requires a passion for doing the right thing and being the best you can be. It requires a passion for helping others along their journey to be the best they can be. Indeed, leaders should not ask others to be the best they can be unless they are committed to being the best *they* can be.

Commitment is also about being loyal to people on the team and being there for others when they fail or when they need your help. Commitment does *not* mean blind loyalty—doing the right thing always trumps loyalty.

I once had an executive say to me, "When they want us to do good they ask us to have integrity, and when they want us to do bad they ask us to have loyalty."

How sad.

Commitment is having the moral courage to do the right thing regardless of friendships or other alliances. Moral courage is an inner strength, the will to listen to the inner voice of conscience and the will to do the right thing even if it is unpopular or comes with personal risk. Moral courage is the resolve to subordinate anything that gets in the way of doing the right thing.

Martin Luther King Jr. put moral courage in perspective when he stated, "The ultimate measure of a man is not where he stands in moments of comfort and convenience, but where he stands in times of challenge and controversy."

FAKE IT TO MAKE IT

I have had managers tell me that there are people they work with whom they do not even *like*—how can they muster up the effort to *love* them?

My response is to tell them to fake it to make it. Don't worry about the feelings—practice the *behaviors* of love (leadership).

C. S. Lewis remarked, "Do not waste time bothering whether you 'love' your neighbor; act as if you did. As soon as we do this we find one of the great secrets. When you are behaving as if you loved someone, you will presently come to love him."

Not long ago I was working with eighty managers from an extremely dysfunctional organization, and partway through my discussion about love, a young woman raised her hand. I called on her, and she said, "I get it. I know what you're trying to do here with us. You're trying to get us to all start liking each other more, aren't you?"

"No, that's not it!" I quickly replied. "I am not trying to get you to *like* each other. I am trying to get you to *love* each other. I'm not concerned with how you *feel* about each other, but I am concerned with how you *behave* toward each other. Forget about the feelings and for now focus on how we are treating each other. You will find that the feelings will follow later."

CHAPTER FIVE

On Hugging and Spanking

I love you. . . .
I'm your biggest fan!

JACK WELCH TO JEFFREY IMMELT

You just had the worst year in the company. . . .
I'm going to take you out if you can't get it fixed.

JACK WELCH TO JEFFREY IMMELT

PETER DRUCKER WAS ONCE ASKED HOW HE WOULD DEFINE people skills in the workplace. His simple reply? "Good manners."

In this chapter, I am going to further develop two of the character skills discussed in chapter 4, namely kindness and honesty or, in business speak, people skills and accountability. My experience is that these are the places where most leaders lose their balance.

I often receive calls from human-resources people who are frustrated and desperate: "Come quick, Mr. Hunter! Our managers and supervisors are train wrecks when it comes to people skills. Please help us teach them some interpersonal skills. Please come quickly!"

When that happens, I love to respond by saying, "Your supervisors have fine people skills!"

There will be silence at the other end before a predictable response of "How can you say that? You don't even know our people. Why, you've never even been here!"

"That's right," I will quickly respond. "But I'll bet you your paycheck that I could take all of your managers with 'bad people skills' and put them into an environment where there are some important people, like an executive cocktail party or a training session, and what do you think I will observe? That's right: wonderful, respectful, kissing-up behavior all day long. Your folks know how to behave. They have just developed a bad habit of behaving poorly with folks they do not think are really important. And your organization has allowed that bad behavior to exist and continue. Now, *that* is something we can go to work on."

I am convinced that we should videotape the interview process of every new hire in our organizations so we can show the tape to them after a year or two on the job. "Say, Darlene, isn't that you on the video? Look how nice you were! Look at the wonderful interpersonal skills you displayed that day. If you look closely, you will see you are even smiling a little! See, we know you can do it—we know you have the skills! Whatever happened to that person?"

When coaching Gestapo-style, insensitive managers, I often say, "Just work on being kind for a while. I know you know how to do it. I could ask your spouse or significant other what you were like back when you were kissing up and trying to impress them. They would tell me all about the sweet, loving, kindhearted, well-mannered, good-listening, thoughtful person you were back then. That's the person we need you to be as the leader."

George Washington Carver said we should be kind to others: "How far you go in life depends on your being tender with the young, compassionate with the aged, sympathetic with the striving, and tolerant of the weak and strong. Because someday in life, you will have been all of these."

ARE YOU LISTENING?

Our definition of kindness in chapter 4 included giving attention to others. Far and away the greatest opportunity we have every day to pay attention to others is in how we choose to listen.

Are you a good listener? Many of us believe we are pretty decent listeners, but the reality is that most of us are rather poor listeners. The majority of people, if they bother to listen at all, listen selectively, thinking, "When is Bob going to stop talking so I can give him the right answer?" or "When is my son going to stop talking so I can give him my autobiographical response?" or "How can I manipulate this conversation around to the way I want it to go?"

Will Rogers once said that if we didn't know it was our turn to talk next, nobody would listen. I don't know if that is true or not, but I do think the good Lord gave us two ears and one mouth for a reason.

Empathic listening is the skill, the discipline, of extending yourself for others by really working to "see it as they see it and feel it as they feel it." It requires kicking all the noise and chatter out of our minds and getting ourselves fully present for what is being said. Empathic listening is hard work, and it requires a great deal of effort.

Listening is an *attitude* toward people. It is developing the willingness, even the desire, to hear people out, better understand them, and learn something new. Has anyone ever learned anything while he or she was talking? Empathic listening is one of the best ways I know to build trust with another human being.

Robert Greenleaf once remarked that "a nonservant who wants to be a servant might become a *natural* servant through a long arduous discipline of learning to listen, a discipline sufficiently sustained that the automatic response to any problem is to listen first. I have seen enough remarkable transformations in people who have been trained to listen to have some confidence in this approach. It is because true listening builds strength in other people."

There is an old saying in leadership circles that everything the leader does sends a message. Think of the sheer number of opportunities we have every day to send a message to people about how much we value or do not value them by how we extend ourselves to really listen to them. When we fail to listen, we are sending messages to those watching and receiving. And none of those messages is coming out to our advantage.

The good news is that empathic listening is an acquired

skill that can be developed over time. Good listening skills are not something we are born with. If you doubt that statement, ask yourself this: Have you ever met a two-year-old who is a good listener?

One of the most powerful dynamics of human interaction is when people feel as though they have been heard. Really heard. Hearing someone does not mean we necessarily have to agree with what has been said. Rather, it is working to understand where people are coming from and then going to a new place together. Dr. Joyce Brothers has commented that listening, not imitation, is the sincerest form of flattery.

When working with executives on the discipline of active and empathic listening, I often have them meet with groups of employees to practice. Their assignment, unknown to the groups, is to just listen to what the employees have to say. They are not to make excuses, defend themselves or the organization in any way, or make any comments at all, with the exception of asking for clarification if it is needed. Any responses to what is said are for another meeting at another time.

The effect of a simple assignment like this is generally enormous. The employees leave making comments like "Boy, we really got some things off our chests," or "That was the most productive meeting with an executive we have ever had here." Remember, the executives did not fix anything! The executives invariably leave feeling better about themselves and their people, having learned much more than they ever knew before.

Listening skills are crucial in developing healthy relationships. Dr. Karl Menninger described listening this way: "Listening is a magnetic and strange thing, a creative force. The friends who listen to us are the ones we move toward, and we want to sit in their radius."

I used to hate going to social functions and boring gatherings like cocktail parties until someone gave me a huge piece of advice that works magically. In fact, it works whenever you are around other human beings. It takes off all the pressure.

Are you ready for this profound piece of wisdom?

Forget about being interesting, and work on being interested.

Works like a charm every time.

ACCOUNTABILITY

I often ask managers in my training sessions this question: "If you do not hold your people accountable to the standards set by your organization, are you honest?"

Most will agree the answer is no.

In fact, if we fail to hold people accountable in the workplace, we run the risk of being both thieves and liars! Sound a little strong? When we fail to hold people accountable, we are stealing from the folks who pay our wages because they pay us to hold people accountable. Not only that—we are in effect lying to those around us because we are pretending that everything is okay, and everything is *not* okay. Remember, honesty means to be free from deception.

Who benefits when the manager does not hold people accountable? Certainly not the employees, because they will not be better off when they leave than when they got there. In fact, they will probably be worse off because they, like the rest of us, are moving in a direction, either getting better or getting worse. The organization certainly does not benefit, although the competition probably will. About the only one who benefits is the manager, because he or she doesn't have to deal with it and can avoid the hassle.

Just think how self-serving and dishonest that is! Someday, an honest leader may follow this self-serving manager, and now the employee can discount the truth: "They've told me I'm great around here for ten years, and now you're telling me I'm not? *You* must be the problem!"

Think of all the excuses we give ourselves for not doing the right thing with people and holding them accountable for their actions. Excuses like "Bill might quit, and it's hard to get people these days," or "Sue is such a nice person and is so helpful with certain things," or "Pete is an intimidating guy," or "Gina gets so defensive whenever I give her any feedback," to name a few.

Children as well as adults have a *need* to know what the boundaries and expectations are and to be held accountable for right actions and right behavior. I know I need friction, and my wife provides a lot of it! She does it because she loves me and wants me to be the best I can be. When leaders fail to meet that need in their people, they are selfishly robbing their people of one of the things they *need* the most.

We should never think we are doing anyone, except ourselves, any favors when we do not hold people accountable and push them to be their best.

Take parenting, for example. Do we benefit our children by accepting mediocrity? Do we help them by allowing them to get by doing the bare minimum? Remember what Vince Lombardi said: "My love will be relentless!" We should never talk about how much we care for those we lead if we are avoiding the hassle of confronting them with any gaps between the set standards and their actual performance.

I often tell managers that they should feel insulted when someone performs below standards, breaks rules, or behaves irresponsibly in their presence. Why? Because the employee doesn't *expect* you to do anything about it! What a message of disrespect. When employees do not perform according to set organizational standards, they are also expecting *you* to behave dishonestly by not doing anything about it.

Says retired general and current secretary of state Colin Powell, "Ironically, by procrastinating on the difficult choices, by trying not to get anyone mad, and by treating everyone equally 'nicely' regardless of their contributions, you'll simply ensure that the only people you'll wind up angering are the most creative and productive people in the organization."

We discipline (train) because we care about people, because we want them to be the best they can be, and because it is our responsibility as the leader. Remember, that is what we signed up for. Richard Green, president of the lip-care company Blistex, flatly states, "It is immoral not to fire those who can't do the job."

He has a point. Think how much is at stake when we fail to take action with poor performers. Think of the bad messages we send to everyone watching about our lack of commitment to excellence and our failure to do the right thing. In addition, many, many people — including spouses, sons, daughters, customers, and vendors — are counting on your organization to provide for their futures. Think of the risk to the organization if you allow poor performance.

Let there be no mistake. In business, the winning formula is simple: Profit equals revenues minus costs, and if there is no profit, the organization will not survive. It is a war in the marketplace, and there are winners and losers. Organizations do fail, people do lose their jobs, and lives are turned upside down.

There is a lot at stake.

DISCIPLINE MEANS TO TEACH

I have been helping organizations implement the principles of servant leadership for many years. Part of that process, discussed fully in chapter 8, involves getting leaders feedback so they can better define the gaps between where they are as leaders versus where they need to be.

Far and away the biggest gap we find in leadership skills is failing to confront people with problems and situations as they arise and to hold people accountable. The second-place gap is not even close.

I have become convinced that much of the anxiety and fear managers have about discipline and confronting people come from a bad paradigm about what discipline really is supposed to be.

Discipline comes from the same root word as *disciple*. Disciple means to teach or to train, which is the proper view of discipline. Discipline is not about punishing or humiliating people. It is simply identifying the gaps between set standards and actual performance and developing a plan to close those gaps. Discipline should be viewed as an opportunity to "disciple" people and get them on the right track and to help them be the best they can be. It need not be an emotional or volatile event if the leader is in control of him- or herself.

Well-known Michigan clergyman Mark Buhr sums up these thoughts brilliantly: "Discipline without love can easily become abuse, while love without discipline is not love at all."

HUGGING AND SPANKING

The most effective servant leaders I know have the extraordinary ability to show unrelenting toughness and sincere affection for people. They can be extremely demanding in their quest for excellence but show equal passion for demonstrating care and love for their people. In short, effective leaders have developed the skill of "hugging" people when they need a hug and "spanking" them when they need a spank.

Most managers fall off the horse one way or the other. Either they are "taskmasters" with little regard for the "soft" skills or they are "wimps" who want everybody to be "happy" and define leadership as a lack of conflict within the group.

Jack Welch, former CEO of General Electric, has been getting some rough press lately, but it is difficult to challenge some of the amazing accomplishments he had at GE. Under his leadership, GE created several hundred *billion* dollars in shareholder wealth, to name one of his more obvious accomplishments. Investor Warren Buffett calls Welch "the Tiger Woods of management." Welch was a master at hugging hard and spanking hard, and examples of both of those traits have become legend at GE.

In reflecting upon how he agonized before he retired over the selection of his successor, which came down to three men, he said, "I love all three of these guys." Few doubt he really meant what he said. Those are just not the kind of words you hear often in boardrooms.

Yet several years before, one of these final three men, Jeffrey Immelt, had a bad year at GE Plastics Americas, which was Immelt's responsibility. Welch took Immelt aside after year end and said, "Jeff, I'm your biggest fan, but you just had the worst year in the company. . . . I love you, and I know you can do better. But I'm going to take you out if you can't get it fixed."

Apparently, current General Electric CEO Jeffrey Immelt got it fixed.

YOU CAN HAVE IT BOTH WAYS

During the 1970s and early 1980s, when "the Big Three" were producing a lot of junk cars, the mantra in Detroit became "quality, quality, quality."

Managers in my quality-circles groups would get so frustrated that they would shout out, "What do you want, quality or quantity?"

The answer?

"We need both, grasshopper."

Now, here it is, more than twenty-five years later, and managers are shouting, "What do you want from us? Nice guy servant leader, or someone who gets the job done?"

Of course, the answer is the same.

Servant leadership and getting the job done are not mutually exclusive. The goal is accomplishing our tasks while simultaneously building our relationships. To accomplish this requires well-developed skills, and there are many organizations paying big bucks to people who possess those skills.

Yes, you can have it both ways. Effective leaders are able to handle the ambiguities inherent in hugging and spanking.

LEADERSHIP AND LOVE: A SUMMARY

One must believe in the leader and believe that his or her word can be trusted. Some have called this the First Law of Leadership: "If you don't believe in the messenger, you won't believe the message." Adds Peter Drucker, "The final requirement of effective leadership is to earn trust. Otherwise there won't be any followers — and the only definition of a leader is someone who has followers."

We spend tons of time, effort, and money developing fancy mission and value statements in organizations today. As important as a mission statement can be in an organization, it means little if folks do not trust the leadership.

Never forget: Once the troops buy into the leader, they'll buy into whatever mission statement the leader's got.

Leadership is about choices. Leadership is choosing to do the right thing day by day, hour by hour, choice by choice — until it becomes habit.

It is the right thing to do to be patient, kind, humble, respectful, selfless, forgiving, honest, and committed. I have never had anyone argue that point at any time, in any part of the world. These principles are self-evident and are the qualities not only of love but of leadership and character.

Effective leaders know that solid character is essential to leadership, and they work diligently to make the right choices, day by day, over and over and over, until they become ingrained habits. Effective leaders understand that they are becoming something different every day by the choices they make. Remember the Chinese proverb "If you do not change your direction, you will end up exactly where you are headed"? Where are you heading today?

There are no human beings, only human becomings. We are all becoming something. As the farmers like to say, "You're either green and growin' or ripe and rottin'." Pick one, because nature shows us in spades that nothing stays the same.

C. S. Lewis makes this point well when he says that "every time you make a choice you are turning the central part of you, the part of you that chooses, into something a little different from what it was before. And taking your life as a whole, with all your innumerable choices, all your life long you are slowly turning this central thing either into a heavenly creature or into a hellish creature. . . . Each of us at each moment is progressing to the one state or the other."

Leadership begins with a choice, and that choice is made when we signed up to be the leader. Now we need to make another choice. Are we going to love (the verb) the people entrusted to our care? If the answer is "Yes!" then we must get prepared to serve and sacrifice because one cannot love people (by definition) without serving and sacrificing for them. When we serve and sacrifice for others, we build authority (influence), and when we build authority with people, we begin earning the right to be called the leader.

The greatest leader is the greatest servant, the one most dedicated to meeting the needs out there in a hurting world full of needs.

And there are many great servant leaders out there. But don't just look to the top of an organization when you search for them. They are often found serving coffee on airplanes, cleaning out bedpans, cooking dinner in kitchens, and hitting baseballs to kids after school.

SO HOW DO I BECOME A SERVANT LEADER?

It is ironic to me that the skills we discussed in the past two chapters are often called "soft skills" in business circles. The truth is that learning management skills is easy and painless compared to developing the skills of leadership.

It is much easier to teach someone how to read a balance sheet than how to become an empathic listener if he or she has had poor listening skills for the past forty years. Teaching a manager the principles of asset management is a piece of cake compared with getting him or her to hold people accountable if he or she hasn't done that for twenty years. Which do *you* think would be more difficult: instructing a manager in a Six Sigma quality system or getting the same type A manager to display patience and humility after a twenty-five-year career of behaving as a command-and-control dictator?

Soft skills?

This is the hard stuff, folks.

We have spent five chapters defining what good leadership looks like, and it is a very high standard indeed. I am certain you agree with most of what has been stated, because the principles are self-evident and timeless.

But intellectual agreement is not enough. As you will recall from what was stated earlier in this book, head knowledge without application is mostly worthless. The effort required to be an effective servant leader is enormous. Yet it can be done, has been done, and is being done effectively by thousands today.

I will spend the remainder of this book detailing the steps necessary to becoming an effective servant leader.

Again, the good news is that we have the technology of how to build servant leaders.

The only question is, are you ready to do the work?

CHAPTER SIX

On Human Nature

Two things fill the mind with ever new and increasing admiration and awe . . . the starry heavens above and the moral law within.

IMMANUEL KANT

BEFORE DISCUSSING HOW PEOPLE CHANGE, BUILDING character, and the steps necessary to becoming an effective servant leader, I believe it is important to first understand human nature and some of the obstacles people face on their journey toward change and growth. Awareness and insight are crucial to change, as will be discussed later.

For many years, I have taught the principles of servant leadership from the United States to Australia, from Mexico to Scotland, from Canada to Singapore. In all of these years, I have yet to have an audience participant raise his or her hand and disagree with the eight principles of love and leadership. As I have said repeatedly in this book, the principles of servant leadership are self-evident. I am convinced that there is a reason why these principles resonate with so many people and why they are self-evident. To better understand human nature and the universality of these principles, I believe it is important to make a distinction between the relativism of values, morals, and ethics and the unchanging nature (law) of principles.

Here is what I mean . . .

VALUES, MORALS, AND ETHICS

Loosely defined, values are those things we consider or rate highly, prize, esteem, or deem important. What ideals and behaviors an organization embraces and deems important— its values—can vary greatly. Think of the values of organizations like the KKK, the Red Cross, Hell's Angels, and the Roman Catholic Church. Organizations and individuals all have value systems, sometimes deplorable ones, and these values guide and shape individual behavior.

The same can be said of morals and morality, which concerns itself with standards of right and wrong. Moral issues deal with conforming to a standard of right ideals and right behavior and are often defined by religious or cultural beliefs and practices.

The world is a very diverse place, and various cultures have very different morals and values that define what is considered right and wrong. These morals and values can range from the morality of a caste system to the number of women a man may marry, from the value of a sacred cow roaming in the streets to the morality of a prearranged marriage, from nakedness in the Congo to the burkas worn in a Muslim country. Obviously, moral behavior in one society can easily be viewed as immoral in another.

Morality even changes over time within a culture, as evidenced in the United States over the past hundred and fifty years. We have gone from legal slavery to the Thirteenth Amendment, from "men-only" suffrage to the Nineteenth Amendment, from prohibition to the Twenty-first Amendment, and from legal racial discrimination to the Civil Rights Act of 1964.

Ethics, then, can be defined as performing or behaving according to accepted standards of conduct and becomes a system for applying our morals, values, and duties.

Now, back to my original point. I have never had an audience participant disagree with the principles of love and leadership discussed earlier. Imagine someone raising his or her hand and saying, "I disagree with honesty," or "Respect and kindness are not appropriate ways to behave," or "Holding people accountable is bad for an organization."

In summary, values, morals, and ethics vary greatly among culture and over time. Principles, on the other hand, are self-evident. But why are they self-evident?

PRINCIPLES

My dictionary defines principles as "comprehensive and fundamental laws." Unlike values, morals, and ethics, which vary greatly between cultures and change over time, principles are unchanging.

We have principles applying to the physical universe that we often refer to as the "laws of nature," such as the laws of physics, geometry, and chemistry.

Similarly, there are "laws of human nature" that apply to the natural laws governing human effectiveness and proper human conduct. The difference, of course, lies in the fact that we are *not* free to disobey the laws of nature (e.g., gravity), but we *are* free to disobey the laws of human nature.

The degree to which we choose to deviate from the laws (principles) of human nature is the degree to which we get off course and begin to run aground. As Cecil B. DeMille, director of the classic *The Ten Commandments,* observed of the principles contained in those great commandments, "It is impossible for us to break the law. We can only break ourselves against the law."

I believe there is substantial proof to support this claim.

Consider a society in which the opposites of the principles we have discussed were valued. Imagine, if you can, a society that valued impatience, incivility, arrogance, selfishness, disrespect, unforgiveness, dishonesty, and little or no discipline. Would that be a society worth living in?

If you study the Bible, Aristotle's *Ethics,* the Koran, the analects of Confucius, or virtually any of the world's religions you inevitably encounter basic principles such as integrity, respect for human life, self-control, honesty, courage, commitment, and self-sacrifice. We may disagree from culture to culture about how many wives a man should have, but most everyone agrees that he should not have another man's wife.

Indeed, the great religions of the world all support this notion of universal human principles. In the epilogue of his classic work *The Religions of Man,* Huston Smith writes, the relationship between the world's great religions and ".... the question of the relation between religions is that in an important respect they are the same. Does not each contain some version of the Golden Rule? Do they not all regard man's self-centeredness of the source of his troubles and seek to help him in its conquest?"

How do we want to be treated by our leader? Do we want a leader who is kind, humble, respectful, selfless, forgiving, honest, patient, and committed? Of course we do. Therein lies the great wisdom of the Golden Rule as it applies to leadership: Be the leader you want your leader to be.

Martin Luther King Jr. spoke about this law of human nature: "There is a law in the moral world—a silent, invisible imperative, akin to the laws in the physical world—which reminds us that life will work only in a certain way. The Hitlers and the Mussolinis have their day, and for a certain period they may wield great power, but soon they are cut down like the grass and wither as the green herb."

So we arrive at another disconnect: If we can all agree on generally acceptable principles of human conduct, why do we so often choose to behave contrary to that standard?

To understand the answer to this question, we need to go even deeper and explore human nature, our moral sense, and character.

HUMAN NATURE

M. Scott Peck, bestselling author and psychiatrist, is often asked in his seminars, "Dr. Peck, what is human nature?"

When asked, Peck will act as if he has never been asked this question before, looking to the ceiling as if pondering the question in depth, before whipping off his reading glasses and blurting out, "Human nature is going to the bathroom in your pants! Next question, please."

Once the audience gets over their shock, he explains his answer.

To two-year-olds, defecating in their pants is a very natural behavior. In fact, what their mother is now proposing seems totally preposterous and unnatural: "What, Mommy? You want me to get up on that big, cold, white thing and do what? No way, Mommy, that's unnatural!"

This is Peck's point. The glory of being a human being, and what separates us from the animal kingdom, is that we can teach and discipline ourselves to do what is not natural until it becomes "second nature." What is "natural" about brushing your teeth in the morning? Have you observed any animals doing that lately? What is "natural" about reading and writing, displaying good manners, or extending yourself for others? Indeed, any time we discipline ourselves to do anything, we are doing what is not "natural" until it becomes "second nature."

Unlike human beings, animals are tightly bound by instinct. When animals receive a stimulus from the environment, they respond according to this programmed instinct.

Of course, animals can learn a conditioned response and repeat an established pattern of behavior, which is why we can teach Shamu to jump over the wire at Sea World. But Shamu certainly cannot take any credit for the training. We are not sure he is even aware of what is happening except that he will get a bellyful of fish at the end of the trick!

As I write this, the monarch butterflies are migrating from the northern and central United States to winter in the mountains west of Mexico City. Some have even been known to fly up to two thousand miles, which is a marvelous feat. But I do get a little crazy when I hear people getting all emotional about the migration, declaring notions about "the glory and wisdom of the monarch!"

Why do monarch butterflies migrate to the mountains outside of Mexico City? Because that is what monarchs do! There is absolutely no freedom to choose the destination of their journey. There is absolutely no decision to be made. The head monarch butterfly is not free to declare one year, "Hey gang, let's fly to Santa Barbara instead this year. We haven't been to the ocean in centuries!" A blue jay in Michigan makes the same kind of nest as a blue jay in California. Again, there is no freedom in the behavior.

Unlike animals, human beings are not tightly bound by instinct and, in fact, have relatively few "natural" instincts. Even the few instincts that some could argue human beings possess, such as survival or procreation, can be transcended, as evidenced by martyrs and celibates.

Human beings are endowed with unique capacities

like imagination, free will, conscience, and self-awareness. Human beings have the unique ability to "ponder their condition" and even make changes to what comes "naturally." Indeed, human beings have the unique ability to *choose* to be different from their nature. Think of the awesome responsibility of having this freedom. When it comes to the kind of person one *is,* that person alone is responsible to determine what he or she will become, what he or she will make out of his or her life.

In a great scene from the classic movie *The African Queen,* Charlie Allnut (Humphrey Bogart) crawls out from below-decks of the boat clearly sporting a nasty hangover. Trying to justify himself after his drunken, rowdy evening the night before, Charlie sheepishly declares to Rose (Katharine Hepburn) that his behavior was only human nature. Not missing a beat, Rose glares at him over the top of her open Bible and snaps back: "Nature, Mr. Allnut, is what we are put into this world to rise above."

MORE ON HUMAN NATURE

A couple of years ago, I attended a large leadership conference where a well-known speaker was presenting the keynote address.

The speaker said this at the end of her lecture: "The Dalai Lama teaches us that the essence of human nature is goodness. We must all remember these words of wisdom on our journey."

The audience broke into spontaneous applause with

those feel-good words. I, however, was left scratching my head in the back of the auditorium, wondering when Paul Harvey was going to jump on the stage and tell us the rest of the story.

The essence of human nature is goodness?

I don't have to look any further into human history than the twentieth century—during which human beings slaughtered more than 100 million people on the orders of Hitler, Stalin, Mao, and Pol Pot in the killing fields — to know there is more than just "goodness" going on in some folks' hearts. I don't have to look any further than September 11, 2001. Indeed, I don't have to look any further than my own heart to know there is more than just goodness going on in there. I have a two-year-old wrapped up in chains down there who I have to watch out for. Sometimes that little guy sticks his head up wanting "me first," and I have to bang him back into place. My wife can tell you all about that little tyrant. As C. S. Lewis said earlier, we have the potential to be heavenly or hellish creatures. Which one gets actualized, which person we become, depends upon our decisions, not our conditions.

Orthodox Christianity has long addressed this predisposition for evil in human beings, referring to it as the "doctrine of the depravity of man" in some circles and "original sin" in others.

Interestingly, scholars from the fields of psychology, philosophy, and sociology are more and more frequently coming to this same conclusion. In talking about the heinous acts perpetrated on September 11, Robert I. Simon, clinical professor of psychiatry at Georgetown University School of Medicine, said, "The capacity for evil is a human universal. There is a continuum of evil, of course, ranging from 'trivial evils' like cutting someone off in traffic, to greater evils like acts of prejudice, to massive evils like those perpetrated by serial sexual killers. But within us all are the roots of evil."

People are often amazed that the human race can even produce such twisted and evil beings as Hitler, Pol Pot, Saddam Hussein, or Stalin. To me, the fact that there are human aberrations like these should not surprise us because we see deformities, abnormalities, and anomalies in nature. What *is* astounding is how these wicked men could get the thousands of human beings behind the scenes to carry out their evil plots.

This potential for good and evil in us all is expressed well in an old Zen Buddhist story. A rather raucous and arrogant samurai once challenged a Zen master to explain to him the difference between evil and good. The master responded disgustedly, "I will not waste my time with such scum as you." With this response, the samurai flew into a rage, unsheathing his huge sword and screaming, "I will cut you into pieces for your insults." "That," the Zen master calmly replied, "is what evil is like." The samurai calmed upon hearing and understanding the wisdom of what the Zen master had spoken. "Thank you for your insight, good master," the samurai humbly replied. "And that," said the master, "is what goodness is like."

Those of you who have had the privilege of raising a two-year-old know all too well of this dual capacity in human beings. Remember the essence of a two-year-old? "Me first! Pooh on you."

Ponder this thought.

Did anyone ever have to teach their kids to be bad?

DO WE HAVE A MORAL SENSE?

Yes, I do believe human beings have an innate, moral sense of right and wrong.

However, to say human beings have a natural moral sense is far different from saying human beings are innately good.

Our moral sense of right and wrong must compete with other senses, desires, and temptations that are just as "natural" to human beings. These urgings may include acquiring possessions, indulging in sex without commitment, desiring pleasure, accumulating power, amassing wealth, and a host of other "natural" desires.

Simply put, our moral sense competes with that little two-year-old who wants it his or her way. How that drama is played out between what we know to be right and how we choose to behave is how our character is forged. More on that later.

Recently, I was teaching servant leadership at the United States Air Force Academy and participated in an ethics workshop. The facilitator set out some interesting scenarios of moral and ethical dilemmas, such as "Is it morally justifiable to tell a lie to the Gestapo if they ask you if you are hiding a Jew in your attic?" Boy, the group really took off to debating that one.

While this type of intellectual jousting can be interesting and entertaining, I am not sure these exercises do much more than add to the moral relativism and "I'm okay, you're okay" thinking that already exist to a dangerous degree in our society.

The fact is that the vast majority of life is *not* a moral dilemma. I am convinced that most people have at least a reasonably good idea what they ought to do in a given situation. We do have general knowledge of right and wrong and a conscience that can guide us.

The only question is, do we have the *will* to do the right thing?

SUMMARY

So there appear to be at least two truths about human nature.

One, human beings have a unique capacity to make moral choices about the stimuli that the world throws at them. We have the ability to choose our response (response + ability = responsibility). Human beings can choose to be different, to behave contrary to and rise above their natural instincts, appetites, and urgings. Human beings can choose to do what is not natural until it becomes second nature.

Two, human beings have the capacity for good and evil. However, the tendency toward bad behavior is the more natural state and must be resisted. As we well know, the garden not tended soon becomes full of weeds. The will to do the right thing is where intentions and actions meet. And this will to do the right thing must be carefully developed and nourished lest we, too, become like one of the many nasty beings to have roamed the planet.

The good news is that there is a set of psychological traits, a moral muscle if you will, that gives human beings the will, courage, and strength to do the right thing.

This moral muscle, if developed and strengthened over time, enables human beings to put principle ahead of self and to rise above self-interest and immediate gratification. This disciplined moral muscle subordinates those things that get in the way of doing the right thing.

We have a name for this moral muscle.

Its name is character.

CHAPTER SEVEN

On Character and Human Change

Leadership is character in action.
WARREN BENNIS

*Ninety-nine percent of leadership failures
are failures of character.*
GENERAL NORMAN SCHWARZKOPF

CHARACTER IS A WORD THAT HAS BEEN GETTING A LOT OF attention in recent years.

Not long ago, there was fierce debate over the importance of character as it relates to leadership. Some even suggested that personal character has nothing to do with leadership. Were you buying into that idea? If you do not believe character is important to leadership, just ask yourself these questions: Do people of low character have influence with you and inspire you to action? Do you have good relationships with people of low character?

Character is a much-used word, especially around election time, but an often misunderstood concept. To better understand character, we need to first differentiate between character and personality.

PERSONALITY

The word *personality* comes from the Latin word *persona,* originally used to denote the masks worn by theatrical players in ancient Greek dramas and which came to encompass the actor's role as well. Personality could be described as the mask we wear for the world to see.

Most psychologists today agree that one's personality has developed and is pretty well fixed by the age of six. There are many personality profiling systems and other tools available to measure personality and the different temperaments, dispositions, and relational styles. For example, DISC is a well-known tool that measures the four primary relational styles: D for dominance, I for influencing, S for steadiness, and C for conscientious. There is quite a bit of scientific support for these four basic styles, and most of us are a complex combination of all of them with usually two dominant styles. Personality types range from extroverted to introverted, outgoing to shy, type A to type B, aggressive to passive, humorous to dry, resilient to reactive, charming to boring, challenger to negotiator, et cetera.

Personality can include a superficial "social image" that people display, like charm, graciousness, and charisma. However, what you see may not be what you get. We have all known people whose character was not consistent with their personality. As Socrates put it more than twenty-three hundred years ago, "The greatest way to live with honor in this world is to be the person we pretend to be."

Personality has little to do with leadership because leadership is not about *style*. Rather, leadership is about *substance*. Personality deals with style while character deals with substance.

I have met excellent leaders who were right-brained, left-brained, tall, short, fat, thin, articulate, inarticulate, assertive, timid, charismatic, boring, dressed for success, and dressed for failure. Look at the great leaders in history, and you will find a full spectrum of leadership styles ranging from Tom Landry to Vince Lombardi, from General Bradley to General Patton, from Mary Kay Ash to Lee Iacocca, from FDR to Ronald Reagan, and from Martin Luther King Jr. to Billy Graham.

Each had a very different style and personality yet was effective in his or her own unique way.

CHARACTER

Dwight Moody, the nineteenth-century lay evangelist, once remarked, "Character is what a man is in the dark."

The word *character* comes from a Greek verb meaning "to engrave." A person's character, then, is the visible sign of his inner nature. Character is what we are beneath our personality (mask).

As stated earlier, personality is generally set by the age of six, but not so with character. Our character is a moving target that in healthy human beings should continue to grow and develop throughout life. Hence the term *maturity*.

Character is of higher importance than personality, as evidenced by the fact that society does not usually hold people accountable for their personality traits but certainly does hold them accountable for their behavior (character).

Character, then, is something very different from personality. Character is our moral maturity, which is our willingness to do the right thing even when — perhaps *especially* when — it costs us something. In fact, I am not sure it can be an act of character unless it costs us something. Indeed, our true character is revealed when the price of doing the right thing is more than we are willing to pay.

Character is our moral and ethical strength to behave according to proper values and principles. The difficult part of life is not *knowing* what is right but *doing* what is right. Again, our character is our level of commitment to doing the right thing, which explains why leadership is "character in action." Leaders seek to do the right thing.

I don't know about the wars and demons you fight every day, but I have to tell you that I have wars going on in my gut every day. I am constantly fighting battles between what I *want* to do and what I *ought* to do. I war against what I know I should do and the shortcut I may want to take today. As stated before, I regularly war with that two-year-old inside me who wants his way.

Developing character is winning those battles repeatedly, until it begins to become habit.

Remember, anyone can love people he or she likes. Anyone can kiss up to the important people. Even the most despicable people on the planet are capable of that. There is an old saying that you can judge people's character by how they treat people who can do nothing for them. Again, leadership (character) is doing the right thing even when we do not feel like it, perhaps *especially* when we do not feel like it.

Again, the message I hope you will fully internalize is that leadership development and character development are one.

NURTURE AND NATURE

There is little doubt that the good and bad habits that become our character are strongly *influenced* by both heredity and environment. Influenced, yes; determined, no.

We know that identical twins with the same genes and reared in the same environment grow up to become two very different people. Even more dramatic are conjoined twins with the same genes, same environment, and even the same *body* who are often two very unique and surprisingly different people.

The "raw materials" of our genetic personalities and the environment we were subjected to growing up vary greatly from one person to the next. For example, the person who has an outgoing personality coupled with a wonderful, loving, and supportive childhood has distinct advantages over the person who is saddled with a more melancholy personality coupled with an abusive, unloving childhood.

Yet examples abound of people raised in horrible circumstances who chose to rise far above their circumstances, become excellent leaders, and build wonderful lives for themselves and their families. Examples also abound of people who were given everything in childhood and who had every privilege and advantage yet chose to live shameful lives.

Yes, it is true that some of us will have to work harder than others according to the hand we have been dealt and the raw materials we have to work with. Similarly, "natural" or "gifted" athletes, musicians, students, and leaders may have to put in less practice time than others.

We all have predispositions and handicaps that can become obstacles to our character development. Some choose to overcome their obstacles; some choose not to. But in the end, what we are, the person we have become, is to a great extent the result of our choices, past and present. To be sure, our future growth and development requires us to be mature enough to accept this responsibility, because if we are unwilling to accept responsibility for our past, we probably will be unwilling to accept responsibility to create our future.

Our present state is a product of our past and present choices, but it need not be the dictator of our future state. Our future state, our future character, will be determined by the choices we make today and tomorrow.

The good news is that we can choose to be something different, starting today.

CHARACTER IS HABIT

Simply put, character is the sum total of our habits, our personal assortment of virtues and vices.

Character is knowing the good, doing the good, and loving the good—the habits of the mind, the habits of the will, and the habits of the heart. Aristotle wrote, "Moral virtue comes about as a result of habit. . . . We become what we repeatedly do. We become just by doing just acts, self-controlled by doing self-controlled acts, brave by doing brave acts."

As I stated before, we have been teaching character to our little eight-year-old for seven years now. Over and over and over and over again! "Be patient, don't interrupt, be nice, be a good listener, don't be arrogant, think about others, forgive, be honest, follow through," and on and on.

You think it's hard to teach an old dog new tricks? Those "puppies" are pretty rough, too!

In summary, we are creatures of habit, and our choices add up to this being we call "me." The ancient adage says it well: Thoughts become actions, actions become habits, habits become our character, and our character becomes our destiny.

Put another way, character may determine our fate (destiny), but character is not determined by fate.

Our character is determined by our choices.

BUILDING CHARACTER

Traditionally, character was built upon the three-legged-stool metaphor. One leg represented the home, where children learned and internalized moral beliefs and moral habits through years of loving discipline. The second and third legs of the stool represented the local school and the local community, where students or members were held to high behavior standards.

For many decades, it seemed as though everyone was pretty much on the same page. Getting in trouble at school or next door probably meant getting it worse at home.

Teaching and assisting our children in developing their character habits is one of the very best gifts parents can impart to their children. As psychologist William James put it, "Could the young but realize how soon they will become mere walking bundles of habits, they would give more heed to their conduct while in the plastic state. . . . Every smallest stroke of virtue or of vice leaves its ever so little scar." Aristotle agreed: "The habits we form from childhood make no small difference — rather, they make all the difference."

We praise talent in this country and reward it handsomely. Yet I am convinced that excellent character is much more to be recognized and praised than talent.

Why? Many of the outstanding gifts that people possess are to an extent — sometimes to a great extent — "God-given" or natural talents and abilities. A well-developed character, on the other hand, is a unique person forged out of his or her own raw material, however flawed or damaged, choice by choice, day by day, year by year. A unique person molded through hard work, courage, commitment, and making the right choices even when those choices were difficult or unpopular.

MY FRIEND ELIZABETH

I would like to close this section on character by sharing a personal experience I will never forget.

One of my favorite people on the planet died a couple of years ago. Her name was Elizabeth Morin, a wonderful elderly woman whom my wife and I chose as our "adopted" grandmother many years ago.

Elizabeth was eighty-nine when she died but was one of the most alive people I have ever known. She was not cynical about the world nor did she think she had "arrived" and had everything figured out. She was always open to new ideas and ways of doing things. She was a quiet woman, even shy, but when she did speak, people who knew her well would listen closely because she would often make wise, even profound, comments. The trouble was you had to be listening *closely* to catch it.

I went to visit Elizabeth in the hospital when she was dying, and I was quite sad, to say the least. While she was consoling *me,* she said she wanted to share something with me that she had learned about character now that she was dying. It was just like Elizabeth to give me a gift before she went home.

The discussion went something like this: "Jim, now that. I am dying, my old friends are all coming to see me."

"Yes, I know, Elizabeth — people have been waiting in line halfway down the hospital corridor for days now."

She thought for a moment and then said something I

will never forget: "Jim, you know, my older friends are like they were when they were younger, only more so."

Did you catch that?

Since I had not been listening *closely* enough either, I had to ask, "What do you mean, Elizabeth?"

"Well, those of my friends who were selfish and self-centered thirty years ago — well, you ought to see them now. They come in my room, sit by my bed, talk about themselves and their problems for ninety minutes, and then leave. I am left wondering why they came.

"But the ones who were on a good path thirty years ago? The ones who cared about others and gave of themselves? You should see them now, Jim. Saints."

Green and growing or ripe and rotting.

I sure miss Elizabeth.

The choices we make on a daily basis have not only determined who we are today but are determining who we will be tomorrow. Again, author C. S. Lewis: "That is why the little decisions you and I make every day are of such infinite importance. The smallest good act today is the capture of a strategic point from which, a few months later, you may be able to go on to victories you never dreamed of. An apparently trivial indulgence in lust or anger today is the loss of a ridge or railway line or bridgehead from which the enemy may launch an attack otherwise impossible."

HOW PEOPLE CHANGE

The truth is that there is nothing noble in being superior to somebody else. The only real nobility is in being superior to your former self.

WHITNEY M. YOUNG JR.

I know of no more encouraging fact than the unquestionable ability of man to elevate his life by conscious endeavor.

HENRY DAVID THOREAU

If you have made it this far in the book, I will make the assumption that you are committed to personal continuous improvement. As was stated earlier, by definition you cannot improve unless you change. Not all change is progress, but all progress does require change.

Herein lies the rub.

CAN PEOPLE REALLY CHANGE?

As I work with people desiring to improve their leadership skills, I generally find it useful to first check their paradigms about change.

I find many people have deep-seated beliefs that people really cannot change all that much, if at all. Our culture even has clichés to support this lie like "A leopard can't change its spots," or "You can't teach an old dog new tricks." How many times did we hear Popeye declare, "I am what I am and that's all that I am, I'm Popeye the sailor man!"? What great mantras these clichés are for couch potatoes!

What wonderful excuses for not taking responsibility for our lives, the direction we are headed, and the person we are becoming every day. And by the way, who said you can't teach an old dog new tricks? I think that is rather insulting to dogs, let alone human beings!

If you do not believe that people can really change, I suggest you go to your local library and check out a few of the thousands of books you will find there about how people have changed their lives for good and became something quite different from what they once were. If we do not believe that people can change, we have no business trying to further develop our leadership skills, because this will require us to change.

It is true that change can be uncomfortable and difficult, and some will resist change more fervently than others. Abraham Maslow, the American psychologist made famous by his "hierarchy of human needs" model, reminds us of how powerful safety and security needs are and, once met, how they must be resisted for continued change and growth.

Embracing change does not come "naturally" to human beings. The good news is that accepting, even embracing, change is a *learned* behavior and that it can even become second nature when practiced over time. Difficult and uncomfortable though change may be, the good news is that human beings can, and often do, grow and change for the better.

In summary, we are wrong if we think people cannot change.

However, we are equally wrong if we believe change to be easy.

STEPS TO CHANGE AND GROWTH

I am deeply indebted to Allen Wheelis for the little book he wrote more than thirty years ago entitled *How People Change*. It is a powerful work on human change, and I recommend it to you.

Wheelis's premise in this book is that human change generally flows through four stages: suffering, insight, will, and finally change itself.

Based upon my years of working with leaders and assisting them in their process of growth and change, I have found these stages to be right on target.

Suffering (Friction)

The first stage generally encountered when working with leaders ("students") is what I often call the friction stage, or what Wheelis refers to as "suffering." Most of us need some friction, pain, or discomfort to get us moving out of our comfort zones. Whether it is desired or not, whether it is easy or not, pain is a powerful motivator for change. Says *Seven Habits* author Stephen Covey, "I think the main source of personal change is pain. . . . If you aren't feeling pain, there is rarely enough motivation or humility to change."

For example, it is often pain or uncomfortable symptoms that motivate us to go to the doctor, dentist, psychologist, church, weight-loss clinic, AA meeting, or a variety of other places seeking relief from the discomfort.

To be sure, there are people who experience significant emotional events that forever change the future course of their lives. But these types of changes are rare compared to the vast majority of us who need some friction to move us out of the monotonous inertia of our lives and into change.

As this discomfort (suffering) applies to leadership, there are a host of symptoms that can get people moving in developing their leadership skills. Friction can come from many different sources: a boss who demands leadership-skills improvement, relationship problems, family problems, health problems, receiving 360-degree feedback from subordinates indicating problems, divorce — the list of symptoms is a long one.

Sometimes, when we arrive on the scene, the leader or leadership team is feeling pain or discomfort as described above.

Conversely, there are times when we arrive on the scene because a true leader is providing self-imposed friction by insisting upon personal and/or organizational continuous improvement. As stated earlier, my wife and I tend to work with rather healthy or rather dysfunctional groups.

Insight

Once we have the attention of the student, the second stage is insight and education.

This education includes becoming aware of how his or her behaviors and relational habits are damaging him or her and poisoning his or her relationships. This insight includes getting intellectual agreement that change is possible, provided the student is truly prepared to change and grow. It includes understanding that change is difficult, and without the full cooperation and commitment of the student, there is little point in continuing.

Insight also includes understanding the great freedom that we as human beings have to ponder our condition, explore alternative behaviors, and make the choice to change. Leaders go too far when they say, "I'm just a lousy leader," or "That's just the way I am," or "What's the use?" Although these expressions do define the leaders' past and present states and may define their future, it doesn't necessarily have to be that way.

Insight must include hope for the student. Hope that comes from understanding and believing that change really can and does occur regularly in the real world. Crooks do become solid citizens, alcoholics do go straight, out-of-control, Gestapo-type bosses do change their spots.

What wonderful news!

Will = Intention + Actions

Here we are again, back to choices!

Toward the end of my seminars, I often tell my audiences this: "If you leave this workshop today and do not apply at least one thing you have learned, then we have wasted a lot of valuable time and effort. In addition to that, we have been stealing from your stockholder or whoever paid your ticket, because head knowledge without application is useless. If your stockholder just wanted you to get a 'warm and fuzzy' feeling today and have nothing applied in your life, we could have saved him or her a lot of money by just sending you a DVD of *Little House on the Prairie,* which you could watch in the comfort of your home, feel warm all over, and then go back to work Monday morning with nothing changed." It is of no value to *learn* what is right and then not *do* what is right.

What is needed for change is the absolute commitment on the part of the student. This commitment includes the readiness to change and the willingness to make the efforts necessary to align intentions with concrete actions. This commitment includes the determination to behave differently over and over and over again until new habits emerge.

DO YOU WANT TO BE HEALED?

This commitment and willingness to change can be difficult to determine on the surface. We often do not know how committed people are until the heavy lifting begins. Again, people will *say* the right things, like "Oh, I want to grow and be the best," or "I believe in continuous improvement!" but their *actions* toward becoming something different from what they currently are always betray their true convictions.

In the Bible, a story is told about Jesus approaching a man who had been deathly ill and unable to walk for nearly forty years. Jesus asks this man what I used to believe was a very strange question. He asks the man, "Do you want to be healed?"

When I first read this story, I thought Jesus' question was rather absurd. "Do you want to be healed?" How ridiculous is that! Of course he wants to be healed. Just imagine living a life of infirmity, for goodness' sake. Who wouldn't want to be healed and be fully healthy again?

Since that time, I have learned that there are many who do not want to be healed.

A wise instructor in my wife's psychology training once told her, "When working with a client, always attempt to discover the 'payoff' for their illness."

My wife says she now better understands what her instructor meant by that statement. There are many possible payoffs people receive for their often-chosen state of being. These rewards can include receiving a lot of attention, not having to work for a living, being the recipient of other people's acts of service and kindness, having people feel sorry for them, and many others.

My wife says she has met many, many people in her practice who *say* they want to change and get better, but relatively few make the difficult and necessary changes to achieve what they say they desire.

Similarly, there are many possible payoffs for being an ineffective leader. For example, being ineffective means that leaders do not have to make the enormous efforts required to meet the legitimate needs of others; they can simply sit back and resort to their positional power, which is quick and effortless. In addition, they do not have to admit they have a problem and do not have to endure uncomfortable feedback from others. The list of possible payoffs is an extensive one.

So having the will to change requires much more than good intentions and impressive statements.

Over the years I have been working with management teams in developing their leadership skills, there are always a few people, usually around 10 percent, who have a phenomenal spurt in their personal development. These are the people about whom others will say, "I don't know what happened to Bob, but he's a different guy."

I have always made it my business with these A+ students to further explore their dramatic growth by asking a couple of simple questions: "So tell me, how did you do it? If you had to write the book on how you went from being a dismal leader to being an effective one, what would you say?"

The many leaders I have asked these questions always, and I do mean *always,* have the same response. They look me in the eye and say, "I just decided to do it. I just got sick and tired of the old me. I finally decided to just get on with it."

Do those sound like an ex-smoker's comments? A person who has successfully lost a lot of weight? A person who has finally achieved sobriety? Indeed, Weight Watchers has its members talk about "the last straw," and Alcoholics Anonymous has its members talk of "hitting bottom." It is reaching that point when the individual says to him- or herself, "I have had enough."

That's it. No bells, whistles, and fireworks shooting off. No glorious epiphanies or messages from angels. Just pure unadulterated change the old-fashioned way—"I just decided to do it."

Sound simple?

It usually does to people who have never tried to really change.

Change

When behaviors are practiced consistently over time, real and lasting change can occur.

It is important for those going through the change process to understand there will be starts and stops, leaps and backsliding, more and less. This discourages many of us, because we want it all and now in our immediate gratification culture.

The reality is lasting change usually comes incrementally, and this is true with both good and bad habits. Remember, our bad habits didn't come easily either. You know how it goes: first a beer, then hard liquor, then a joint, then a little coke . . . First a lie, then bigger lies, then a small theft, then a large one, then . . .

Says basketball coaching legend John Wooden, "When you improve a little each day, eventually big things occur. . . . Don't look for the big, quick improvement. . . . Seek the small improvement one day at a time. That's the only way it happens—and when it happens, it lasts."

THE ANATOMY OF A HABIT

William James called human beings "bundles of habits." To further understand the forces at work when one is truly committed to change, it is important to understand the dynamics involved in developing and breaking these habits that have such a tight grip on our lives.

Habits predictably will travel through four stages before becoming the "default" response in our behavior. Let's take a brief look at these four stages.

Stage One: Unconscious and Unskilled

The first stage is the unconscious and unskilled stage, at which we have no knowledge and are oblivious to the skill or behavior. This is pre–potty training; before that first drink or cigarette; before learning to ski, play basketball, play the piano, type, read, write, or become a better leader.

In this stage, you are either unaware or uninterested in the behavior and are therefore unskilled.

Stage Two: Conscious and Unskilled

This is the stage at which we become aware of a new behavior but have not yet developed the skills and habits necessary to perform well on a consistent basis.

This is when Mom first starts suggesting we get on that big white commode (how unnatural, Mommy!); when we smoke that first cigarette, drink that first awful alcoholic drink, fall twenty times the first time we try to ski down the slope, begin playing the piano, learn to type, et cetera.

Stage two is the awkward stage, and this awkwardness must be resisted when we are on our path to growth and improvement. If we do not resist the awkward feelings, we will often give up.

For the leader, this awkwardness may occur when he or she first starts to hold people accountable, starts appreciating people for their efforts, or begins treating *employees* with respect rather than just his or her boss. It can feel awkward, uncomfortable, and even intimidating, and those feelings must be resisted and worked through.

Which is why commitment is so important.

Stage Three: Conscious and Skilled

This is the stage at which we are becoming more and more skilled and comfortable with the new behavior, and it is becoming a skill and even a habit. This is when the child rarely has an accident making it to the bathroom; when the cigarettes or booze are tasting pretty good, snow skiing feels a lot less awkward, and the typist and pianist rarely, if ever, need to look at their fingers on the keyboard anymore.

This is the "getting the hang of it" stage. We still have to think about it to some degree, push ourselves to action, continue practicing, but it's becoming more "natural."

Stage Four: Unconscious and Skilled

The final stage is when we don't have to "think" about it anymore because the behavior has become habit and very natural. Indeed, the behavior has become our "second nature."

Do we have to "think" about brushing our teeth in the morning? I hope not. Does a skilled typist or pianist "think" about which keys to strike?

Stage four is the chain-smoker who has three cigarettes burning in three different ashtrays, the alcoholic, or the skier who goes down the slope as naturally as he or she walks down the street.

Stage four is the leader who doesn't have to *try* to be a good leader because he or she has *become* a good leader.

Habits, both good and bad, take time to develop, and they take time to break. My experience working with leaders and character change is that it takes a minimum of six months to begin extinguishing an old character habit until the new response has become the "default" response. And this is a minimum. We may even struggle with certain serious habits for many years.

SELF-ESTEEM AND CHANGE

I have read works from various authors claiming that self-esteem is essential to growth and change for individuals. If people do not "feel good" about themselves or if their "inner child" is damaged, growth and change rarely follow. So they exhort parents, teachers, and bosses to lavish all kinds of recognition and praise on their subjects, whether they deserve it or not, to nourish their all-important self-esteem.

"I feel good when I do good" was the teaching of Abraham Lincoln, and I have found this to be true in my work.

Self-esteem and confidence are not built by telling

people they are wonderful and competent when they clearly are not. Esteem and confidence come from setting and achieving goals, extending oneself for others, and getting oneself aligned with "true north," as discussed earlier. When people begin to serve others and behave in healthy ways, they begin to see themselves differently and gain confidence as a result. There is ample evidence to support this claim.

In his classic study on altruism, psychologist Ervin Staub studied those who risked their lives protecting Jews from the Nazi regime. Said Staub, "Goodness, like evil, often begins in small steps. Heroes evolve; they aren't born. Very often the rescuers made only a small commitment at the start, to hide someone for a day or two. But once they had taken that step, *they began to see themselves differently,* as someone who helps" (italics added).

As you read further in the study, these "heroes" who "saw themselves differently" began to take more and more risks because they *knew* they had to "help." They were seeking alignment between how they saw themselves (as helpers) and what they were doing to help (their actions).

Interestingly, there is also a widely acclaimed investigation of the rescuers of Jews during the Holocaust that determined that many of these heroic persons actually had *low* self-esteem. In fact, the researchers concluded that there was absolutely no connection between self-esteem and being a rescuer.

Perhaps a surprise to some, recent studies have concluded that certain forms of high self-esteem seem to increase one's proneness to violence and also reveal a strong link between high self-esteem and unethical and antisocial behavior.

I wonder if the extreme arrogance and pride displayed by executives at Enron or Tyco contributed to the unethical and immoral behaviors that investigators are just beginning to uncover.

A more classic example would be many in the German population during the Nazi regime who had a very high regard for themselves as the Aryan race. This high regard became the basis for such atrocities as ethnic cleansing and the Final Solution.

SUMMARY

The good news is that human beings are bundles of habits.

The bad news is that human beings are bundles of habits.

Habits can be changed, and they can be changed for the better. We can choose to be something different than we are today. It is never too late to learn and grow. If you are too old or lazy to learn and grow, then you are too old or lazy to lead.

Changing years of ingrained habits and behaviors requires a great deal of commitment and effort. Unfortunately, many people are simply not up to the task.

For those of you who are committed to the goal of being the best leader you can be, there is a very effective process available that can assist you on your journey.

This is where we now turn.

CHAPTER EIGHT

On Implementation

*We must become the change we
wish to see in the world.*

MAHATMA GANDHI

*The modern workplace can be an extraordinarily
powerful character-building institution. . . . I feel
character is a corporation's most valuable resource
and product. A successful corporation's, that is.*

RALPH S. LARSEN,
FORMER CEO, JOHNSON & JOHNSON

FOR MANY YEARS I TAUGHT THE PRINCIPLES OF SERVANT
leadership to what seemed to me to be eager and appreciative
audiences in public as well as private settings. Managers would
often write glowing evaluations of how they loved the material
and how excited they were to become servant leaders.

Twelve to eighteen months after conducting servant-
leadership training with an organization's management
team, predictably I would receive a phone call from the HR
person saying it was "time to come back and charge everyone up again."

Of course, I was happy to oblige, but after the third or fourth return visit to the same organization, I began to feel badly for the shareholder, taxpayer, or whoever was paying the bill for the training. Again, if all we get from training are nodding heads and good feelings rather than results in the form of changed behavior, just what is the point?

TRANSFER OF TRAINING

As an HR person in my early life, I was well aware of the dim statistics regarding leadership training and the quantifiable results of the training. Studies consistently show that only 10 percent of training is ever actually implemented, what the late educational psychologist Edward Thorndike called the "transfer of training."

Think of the obscene amounts of money spent on leadership training every year around the world. I do not believe too many shareholders or taxpayers would say that change in one out of ten people was a fair return on their investment.

Early on, I believed that this 10 percent figure I had heard so often was unrealistically low, so I began asking some questions about my leadership training to test the numbers. A year or so following leadership training for an organization, I began calling the HR person and asking how many people who went through the training had actually made visible and lasting improvements in their leadership skills, how many were actually "different" as a result of having heard the message.

Humbling and disappointing to me, I discovered the

answer to be very near that 10 percent figure. In a group of fifty managers, the HR person might cite four or five who really had made some significant and noticeable changes in how they were behaving.

I was dumbfounded.

Why weren't people applying what they had learned? Why weren't people changing? Why weren't they implementing the principles they so enthusiastically embraced?

TURNING POINT

Then the teacher arrived (the student was ready), and roughly ten years ago I made a dramatic shift in my approach to training.

I was conducting servant-leadership training for the third time with the same group of managers for an organization in central Indiana. At the end of the seminar, I noticed that one of the men in the front row was literally in tears and had his hand raised.

I will never forget what he said.

"Jim, I believe everything you said today, just like I believed it three years ago when I heard it for the first time. You are preaching to the choir, man. I know better than anyone that I need to be doing this stuff at work, in my marriage, and with my three boys.

"But let me tell you what the problem is, Jim. Let me share with you what will happen when you leave here today and I go back to work. On my desk I have a QS-9000 project I am up to my ears in, I have a departmental budget due by

Friday, I have four late performance reviews I need to write, I have safety issues I need to deal with, I have one problem child I need to step up to, and that is just off the top of my head.

"As far as this training goes, I will probably not hear another word about servant leadership until you come back here again in another year or two. I will not be challenged to apply these principles by upper management, nor will I see upper management practicing these disciplines.

"As ashamed as I am to admit it, this servant-leadership jazz is going to end up on the back burner, just as it has in the past. I come here, get excited, become hopeful, and then *nothing*. This will be the end of it. To be totally honest with you, Jim, I think it is unfair for you guys to even do this to us."

His comments cut me to the core. Of course, he was absolutely correct, and I received my first glimpse into what was missing.

At a minimum, we needed to create an environment for people to talk about these principles on a regular basis. We needed to create an environment in which people were supported and encouraged to grow and develop as leaders. We needed to create an environment in which people were given a little "friction" to grow and a little "push" in their quest for continuous improvement. We needed to get the top levels of management *really* bought into the principles and personally practicing the disciplines for all to see.

Soon after this event in Indiana, I received more insight into what was missing. Along came an author named Daniel Goleman.

EMOTIONAL INTELLIGENCE

Goleman, a Harvard professor and bestselling author, has written a few books about what he calls "emotional intelligence."

Emotional intelligence is a broad term encompassing interpersonal skills, motivation, social skills, empathy, and self-awareness. Five decades ago, Dale Carnegie observed that upward of 75 percent of success in leadership required interpersonal skills, and many scoffed at him. Along comes Daniel Goleman a half-century later, armed with empirical studies and facts, announcing that 80 to 100 percent is needed!

Quoting Goleman: "There is an old-fashioned word for the body of skills that emotional intelligence represents: character."

Goleman studied and reported on the great progress that scientists have made over the past few decades in the field of neuroscience, and I would highly recommend his work to you left-brained folks who would like all the details.

A major premise in Goleman's work is that one does not learn emotional intelligence, leadership skills, or character the way one learns technical or analytical skills like algebra, physics, car mechanics, or how to set up an Excel spreadsheet.

Simply put, leadership is not something you *grasp* intellectually. One does not become a better leader by saying, "Yes, I agree with the principles of servant leadership," because mere intellectual assent means little. As mentioned earlier, *everyone* agrees with the principles!

Much more is needed.

Advances in neuroscience clearly show that the emotional part of the brain, the part where character is developed, learns differently than the thinking part of the brain. Emotional-intelligence skills are developed in a region of the brain called the limbic system, which controls our impulses, motivation, and drives. Technical and analytical skills are learned in the neocortex, which is the part of the brain able to grasp logic and concepts.

Again, leadership is not something to be grasped intellectually—rather, it is analogous to becoming an athlete, carpenter, or musician. Leadership skills are developed by combining knowledge with the necessary actions to become proficient. Again, did anyone ever learn to swim by reading a book?

I often tell my audiences at the beginning of a seminar that they will not become better leaders by attending the seminar. Amazingly, no one has run out the door at that point yet! I say to them, "What if I had advertised this seminar by promising you that after four hours with me you would become a scratch golfer, an accomplished pianist, or a master carpenter? Would anyone have paid money for that? Except for the most gullible among you, probably not.

Reasonable people would say that it is impossible to accomplish that in four hours, and they would be correct."

You can learn *about* leadership reading a book, going to a seminar, or watching a videotape. But you will never *become* a better leader by doing those things. Yet this is exactly how the vast majority of leadership seminars and courses around the world are taught.

Sadly, most organizations do not insist that their vendors of leadership training provide them with what is truly needed in order to get real behavior change. In part, this is because organizations are also guilty of not approaching leadership as a skill needing to be learned, developed, and continually improved over time. It requires much less time, effort, and other resources to just promote someone to supervisor, bump his or her pay 20 percent, send him or her off to a one-day supervisory-skills seminar, shoot a quick memo off informing the family that this person is now one of the parents, and voilà! This person is now fully equipped to lead the organization's greatest asset!

Now, there is good and bad news about human beings developing emotional intelligence (character).

The good news is that emotional intelligence is not fixed genetically, as is IQ, which changes little past our teen years. Emotional intelligence can be developed throughout life, a process referred to as maturity.

The bad news is that it takes a great deal of effort to break old habits and replace them with new habits. Says Goleman, "With persistence and practice, such a process can lead to lasting results. . . . It's important to emphasize that building one's emotional intelligence cannot—will not—happen without sincere desire and concerted effort. . . . But it can be done."

A NEW PROCESS IS BORN

Taking what I learned from that manager in Indiana, Daniel Goleman, and my understanding of building character and changing habits, I developed a simple process to assist people in improving their leadership skills.

This process is based upon a simple quality model I worked with in the early 1980s. This three-step model involved (1) defining the specifications, (2) identifying any deviations from those specifications, and (3) eliminating the deviations.

My thought was, why couldn't this same model, so effective in producing quality products or delivering quality services, be utilized to assist human beings in developing a quality leadership system in their own lives or in their organizations?

THE MAP

Below I will outline how we typically implement this leadership-improvement process with individuals or an entire leadership team.

I want to emphasize that a formal program implemented by a member of our organization is *not* required—any individual or group can apply these principles on their own. I have become convinced, however, that it is necessary to incorporate each of what I call the "three Fs" into the process in order to ensure long-term behavior change.

These three Fs are Foundation, Feedback, and Friction.

Step #1: Foundation (Set the Standard)

When human beings enter a new team environment—whether they are students, employees, children, or athletes—they generally have two basic subconscious questions that the leader needs to answer as quickly as possible.

Question number one: "How am I supposed to behave?"

Question number two: "What happens if I don't behave that way?"

Those in leadership positions need to answer these questions and answer them thoroughly. It is crucial for any top leader who has a vision for excellence in leadership to be able to articulate and communicate that vision.

Organizations must make it clear to aspiring leaders that effective leadership and continuous improvement are *required* behavior if one is going to assume the privilege and awesome responsibility of being the leader. Quality guru W. Edwards Deming said it best: "The first step in a company will be to provide education in leadership."

Those in leadership positions need effective training in the principles of servant leadership to provide them with a solid working knowledge of what good leadership looks like and where they are headed as leaders. As Stephen Covey teaches, "begin with the end in mind."

Toward that end, leaders going through our process begin by attending a four-hour servant-leadership training-and-orientation session. Participants are trained in the principles of servant leadership so that they clearly understand what excellent leadership looks like. In short, the training identifies the standard (foundation) and sets the bar. Of course, there are other ways to set the standard, including seminars, books, videos, tapes, and other learning tools.

Also in this session, a complete orientation is included on how the process will be implemented over the coming months.

Step #2: Feedback (Identify the Gaps)

Following the initial training, Step #2 requires participants to clearly understand their personal deviations from the high standard of servant leadership and their current leadership skills. Simply put, we must identify the gaps between the set standard and current performance.

Several years ago, we developed and have been working to perfect a tool to measure individual leadership skills against the principles of servant leadership. This tool, called a Leadership Skills Inventory (LSI), is conducted anonymously on a 360-degree basis at the start of the process to determine baseline performance and again following six calendar months to monitor changes (see Appendix 1). In addition, LSI self-assessments are also completed (see Appendix 2).

The LSI is a simple tool to administer and can generally

be completed in less than fifteen minutes. It consists of twenty-five statements about the participant along with two open-ended questions. Generally, ten or more LSIs are distributed and completed on each participant by subordinates, peers, superiors, customers, vendors, significant others, family members, and others before the scores are tabulated.

From the inventories, a summary report is generated (see Appendix 3) for each participant, showing strengths and weakness (gaps) in a rank-ordered format to assist the participant in clearly identifying where his or her personal opportunities exist.

It is generally enlightening for people to see their self-assessments juxtaposed against their 360-degree feedback to illustrate how they see themselves versus how the world sees them.

Incidentally, 360-degree feedback is nothing new in the United States — roughly two-thirds of businesses with more than one hundred employees currently use some type of 360-degree format. The difference with this format is that the inventory provides a measurement *specifically* related to the principles of servant leadership discussed earlier.

What most organizations and leaders fail to do with 360-degree feedback is to take the feedback to its logical last step. They fail to require the leader to set specific and measurable plans to begin closing his or her gaps. They fail to set up ongoing accountability to ensure change and continuous improvement.

Step #3: Friction (Eliminate Gaps and Measure Results)

As discussed in the last chapter, creating appropriate "friction" is crucial to change: No pain, no gain.

In order to create friction—a healthy tension, if you prefer—it is important for people to become convinced that the top leadership is fully committed to the process and is expecting to see continuous improvement in the form of growth and behavior change.

To monitor and measure the changes, two SMART (*S*pecific, *M*easurable, *A*chievable, *R*elevant, and *T*ime Bound) action-plan goals are set quarterly by each participant (see Appendix 4). These goals are developed from the feedback received from the LSI summary reports.

SMART action-plan goals could include developing patience and humility, giving respect, showing appropriate appreciation, developing active listening skills, learning confrontation skills, or any of the other character skills detailed in chapters 4 and 5.

Some have questioned why the majority of our focus is placed upon the relationship-oriented facets of leadership rather than the task or technical aspects. The fact is, we used to do just that. Over the years we discovered that we rarely came across managers who were struggling on the technical or task-oriented components of their job. Indeed, their strength in those areas was probably why they were promoted to leadership positions in the first place. Says leadership expert Warren Bennis, "I have never seen anybody derailed, plateaued, fired, or passed over because of a lack of technical competence. But I've seen many people get derailed because of poor judgment and character."

The rationale for all of this madness is to assist people in their change and growth process by taking a two-pronged approach.

The first is to enlighten participants about the behaviors and poor habits that have become obstacles to their being more effective leaders. The second is to assist them in not only eliminating the poor habits but replacing them with healthy habits. These new and healthier habits must be practiced over and over again, month in and month out, until the old habit has been extinguished and the healthy habit becomes the "default" behavior. This practice must continue until the new behavior (skill) becomes unconscious, as discussed earlier.

MORE FRICTION

In addition, each participant appears quarterly before a Continuous Improvement Panel (CIP) to discuss their LSI results and to present their SMART plans and goals. The CIP, which can be facilitated by a member of our organization, is composed of the top decision-maker in the organization, an HR person, and the participant's immediate manager. The purpose of the panel is to provide support and resources and to increase accountability. When a person makes a commitment to change, face to face, in front of the CEO and other key leaders, and he or she knows his or her progress is being measured, the need to take continuous improvement and growth seriously becomes clear and a much higher priority.

To provide further friction, participants are asked to share their LSI summary results *and* their SMART action plans and goals with their peers and subordinates in a group setting. Perhaps you have heard the old saying that if you want to lose ten pounds, tell everyone in your neighborhood what you are attempting to do — they will ask you regularly about your progress! Once shared with peers and subordinates, friction and accountability are greatly enhanced.

Also, immediately preceding the quarterly CIP sessions, we recommend further training sessions to continue to reinforce the foundation. Topics we train on include Community Building, Performance Planning and Review, Constructive Discipline, Character and Professionalism, Empathic Listening and Assertiveness, More on Servant Leadership, et cetera. Whatever format is used, it is important to continually reinforce the principles. Remember, we need to be reminded more than we need to be instructed.

Finally, process participants are given monthly group assignments to practice the disciplines they have been learning. For example, one month the group will get together and each person will take four minutes to share his or her life story. The first goal of the exercise is to be as assertive as possible in the presentation, which means being as open, honest, and direct as possible. The second goal is to get people to "go deeper" rather than talking about their work or merely making small talk. This allows leaders to practice and develop humility and vulnerability, two very important qualities of leadership.

In summary, Step #3 requires the leadership team to create a healthy tension and levels of accountability to ensure follow-through. Our experience shows that when this level of friction is created, there is simply no place to hide. Each participant must make a *choice* (there's that word again) and decide either to change and grow or perhaps leave the organization, because they will become very uncomfortable. Occasionally there are casualties, but we have found this to occur with less than 2 percent of participants. In any event, the choice is one that each individual must make for him- or herself.

ADDITIONAL PROCESS BENEFITS

Over the years that this approach has been evolving and improving, we have discovered a few powerful collateral benefits.

One of these benefits is that the leadership team becomes more connected and a sense of team "community" is always built. Openness, honesty, and vulnerability between team members are *always* enhanced by what is learned and shared, which becomes the foundation for building community on an even higher level throughout the organization.

Also, the evaluation process involves the rank-and-file people in the organization and communicates to them that the leadership team is *truly* committed to continuous improvement and to being the best leadership team possible.

That, in turn, gives the leadership team the *authority* to ask the rest of the organization to strive to be the best they can be.

OTHER THOUGHTS ABOUT THE PROCESS

I never cease to be amazed that organizations do not insist that their leaders be continually improving and persistently working toward becoming the best leaders they can be. With the awesome responsibility of leading others and the high stakes involved, it seems obvious to me that organizations would focus their attention on helping their leaders develop their leadership skills and thereby their character.

I am convinced that one of the greatest opportunities our institutions in America have to "give back" to society is by helping its members to build their character, as stated in Ralph Larsen's quote at the beginning of this chapter. When qualities of character are expectations in the workplace and people are afforded the opportunity to learn and grow, the effects spill out into society.

My most rewarding moments occur when I receive comments and e-mails from spouses and other family members about the changes they see in the person they love. Real changes in character become evident in every aspect of a person's life.

Obviously, this process requires a great deal of individual commitment as well as commitment from the top of the organization. In fact, I generally insist that the top levels of the organization participate in the process, because they need to be growing, changing, and setting an example for all to see. As Margaret Wheatley says, "the higher you are in the organization, the more change is required of you personally."

To be sure, if I have a true commitment from the top of the organization, my job becomes relatively easy. There is a time in every committed organization I have worked with—typically three to four weeks in—when it finally sinks into the collective consciousness of the group: "Wow, we really are committed to this stuff." When that happens, we make rapid progress.

Remember: "How am I supposed to behave?" and "What happens if I don't behave that way?" I am convinced that every organization has a moral obligation to its members, and especially to its leaders, to clearly answer those two questions.

DO I HAVE TO BE PERFECT?

We tell people going into the process that they may be the worst leader in the building—and that that is okay for now. However, the expectation is that they will be working toward getting the slope of their continuous-improvement line moving in a northerly direction.

The goal in developing our leadership skills is not to be perfect. The goal is continuous improvement. Not everyone can be all-American, valedictorian, or top salesperson, but everyone *can* be the best he or she can be. As Coach John Wooden put it, "Perfection is an impossibility but striving for perfection is not."

People going through a change process, like the one

discussed here, need to understand that it will be exciting at times, boring at times, stressful at times, and even painful at times. There will be starts and stops, and some backsliding will probably occur. It is also important to keep in mind that individual change is not an "either/or" or an "all or nothing" proposition. Rather, change and continuous improvement are about "more or less" and "better or worse." It is important to keep encouraging one another and cheering one another on so that people do not get discouraged and give up. It is critical to stay committed and trust that eventually the fruit will come.

We will never "arrive," so the goal is to keep moving forward on our journey so we can periodically declare, "I am not what I want to be, but I'm not what I *used* to be!"

So forget about being perfect. Our society is hard on leaders these days, often expecting them to be all things to all people. People will make mistakes; they will let us down; they will do well for a while, backslide, and go forward again, and all of that is okay. Indeed, it is the human condition.

My favorite Civil War story concerns a rumored incident in which several of Abraham Lincoln's advisers complained about General Grant's drunkenness in the field. Lincoln was quick to remind them of Grant's great battlefield accomplishments and ended the conversation by saying, "Perhaps we should find out what the good general drinks and send a case to every general in the Army."

SUMMARY

There was a time when I believed that the out-of-control command-and-control managers I worked with must just be bad people. I now know that this is rarely the case. Few wake up in the morning and consciously try to spend their day being inadequate leaders. Most parents, bosses, coaches, teachers, pastors, and others I have met, even the struggling ones, have a sincere desire to be good leaders.

What I do find is that many of the people who struggle as leaders have never received the proper education on what good leadership looks like. I usually find that they have not received the necessary feedback to help them keep their balance over time. And I practically never find struggling leaders who have received adequate friction or are held accountable for their change and growth.

If you truly are committed to continuous improvement and becoming an effective leader, I am convinced that each of the three steps described in this chapter must be employed in order to ensure true and lasting behavior change.

You do not need a formalized process (although having one is helpful) nor do you need to hire outside consultants to assist you. However, you must be sure that you have:

1.   **A foundation.** Get educated on the timeless principles of servant leadership and continuously update your knowledge. There are many books, videos, tapes, and other tools available to assist you. Knowing and setting the standard is vital if we are too have any chance of moving towards it.

2.   **Feedback.** Find a way to get feedback from the significant people around you. Be sure you are scratching the right itches and do not assume you know where your gaps lie. Remember, you have been behaving this way for decades and you may well have lost perspective.

3.   **Friction.** Find people who will hold your feet to the fire. This step of eliminating the gaps is crucial and you must work on finding good accountability partners on your journey toward continuous improvement.

Now for some, this process may seem a bit tedious, cumbersome, and even awkward. Believe me, I have attempted, read about, and observed many other approaches yet I do *not* know of a more effective way to get true and lasting behavior change.

What I *do* know from twenty-six years of experience working with leaders is that training alone is not nearly enough. Identifying performance gaps through 360-degree feedback is not enough. Follow-up in the form of friction and accountability combined with training and feedback is the right formula to give you the best shot at change and growth.

Winston Churchill once remarked, "Democracy is the worst form of government except for all those others that have been tried." That is precisely how I feel about this process.

CHAPTER NINE

On Motivation and Other Essentials

You get the best effort from others not by lighting a fire beneath them, but by building a fire within them.

Bob Nelson

MOST WOULD AGREE THAT MOTIVATION IS AN IMPORTANT component of leadership, so I have chosen to spend the last chapter of this book discussing this often misunderstood topic. Later in the chapter, I incorporate bits and pieces of what I refer to as "The Essentials" for the servant leader's toolbox.

Common sense and more than two hundred years of research suggest that human actions are driven by consequences for behavior. Behavior that is rewarded tends to be repeated; behavior that is punished or ignored tends to stop. From these observations, many have deduced that "motivating" people to action through reward and punishment is what motivation is all about. This could not be further from the truth.

KITA

When I ask audiences how a leader motivates people to action, inevitably I get the clichéd response, "Give 'em some good old fashion KITA!" (KITA = *Kick in the A*ft end.)

The "enlightened" side of the audience will look horrified at this primitive response yet will respond with an archaic response of their own. With a hint of superiority, they will preach back, "You certainly do not need to kick people to motivate them. For goodness' sake, this is the new millennium! All you need to do is implement an equitable pay-for-performance plan. That is what really motivates people to action!" With that said, they are off and arguing about which variety of "motivation" works best. Carrot-or-stick discussions can be a lot of fun.

What both sides fail to see in these predictable responses is that they are talking about two different sides of the same coin. KITA can be distributed through positive or negative means in the form of bribes or punishments, but these forms of behavioral manipulations have little to do with motivation.

To illustrate this, let's say that in a moment of weakness, you allow your spouse to buy an ugly white French poodle. One day you see it lying on your favorite chair, and you swat it with the newspaper. The offended poodle yips at you but quickly obliges.

Question: Have you motivated the poodle to get off your chair? I can hear some of you emphatically responding, "You bet I did!"

But the reality is that the only one motivated in this scenario is *you*. You want the poodle off the chair. The poodle would still rather be lying on it and will be again as soon as you leave the house. Did your negative KITA motivate the poodle to get off and *stay* off the chair?

Now, some time has passed, and your spouse has threatened to leave you if you do not stop hitting that precious poodle every time it gets on your chair. So you decide to take an "enlightened" approach and use positive KITA. Now when you catch the poodle on your chair, you bribe it with a crispy piece of bacon, which the poodle willingly jumps off the chair to receive.

Question: Have you now motivated the poodle to get off the chair? The answer remains the same as before.

You are still the only one in the room who is motivated to get the poodle off the chair. The poodle still wants to be there and will be there again in short order.

TRUE MOTIVATION

We cannot begin to talk intelligently about motivation until we understand that true motivation is about lighting a fire *within* people. True motivation is influencing and inspiring people to action and getting their *internal* generator running. Motivation is people moved to action because they *want* to act. They *want* to give their best and their all for the team.

Remember, we cannot change anyone. The best we can do is influence their future choices. Bribes and punishments are short-term fixes that do little to get people's hearts and minds. Peter Drucker puts it this way: "Economic incentives are becoming rights rather than rewards. Merit raises are always introduced as rewards for exceptional performance. In no time at all they become a right. To deny a merit raise or to grant only a small one becomes a punishment. The increasing demand for material rewards is rapidly destroying their usefulness as incentives and managerial tools."

SATISFIERS VERSUS MOTIVATORS

Decades ago, behavioral scientists led by Frederick Herzberg conducted research into behavior motivation on the job.

The behavioral scientists classified their results into two categories, satisfiers and motivators. Almost a half century later, we are still struggling to understand — let alone believe — their findings.

Satisfiers, also called maintenance factors, are those things that people must receive from their employer in order to expend even minimum effort on the job. These satisfiers would include wages, benefits, working conditions, and other basic safety and hygiene factors. Herzberg's team concluded that once satisfied, merely increasing a satisfier does not motivate people to work harder. For example, will employees who are already satisfied with their organization's benefits work harder if their plan now offers veterinary benefits? However, if people are "not satisfied" with one of these maintenance factors, they may not expend even minimal effort.

Motivators, on the other hand, are those factors that

stimulate people to put out more energy, effort, and enthusiasm in doing their jobs.

Motivators include recognition, praise, appreciation, opportunity for growth, challenge, meaningful work, and job satisfaction. Herzberg found that increasing a motivator will stimulate people to give more.

MORE EVIDENCE

You are probably aware of the studies dating back sixty years that show a sharp contrast between what managers *perceive* as being most important to employees and what actually *is* most important to employees. Over the past twenty-five years, at least three other studies have been conducted on the same topic, and all have found remarkably similar results to the older studies.

When asked what employees want from their work, the overwhelming majority of managers say "money," followed by "promotion or growth opportunities," and then "job security." Money is always found at the top of the manager's list.

When employees are asked what they want from their work, these studies consistently show money as no higher than number five on the list and as low as number seven. Other factors like "full appreciation for work done," "feeling 'in' on things," "boss sympathetic to personal problems," and "job security" rate higher than compensation.

In 1996, the National Association of Colleges and Employers conducted a survey on what was most important to students when they entered the workplace.

In order of importance, they were:
- Enjoying what they do
- Using their skills and abilities
- Growing in personal development
- Feeling that what they do matters
- Receiving good benefits
- Receiving recognition for good performance
- Working in a location they like
- Receiving a generous salary
- Working in team-oriented situations

We have been hearing these same things over and over again for decades, but apparently most of us are not listening, refuse to believe it, or are not willing to make the efforts required to meet the higher-level needs and motivators that people have.

As if these empirical studies were not enough, an exhaustive study conducted at Wichita State University by management professor Gerald Graham found that the most powerful motivator is personal, instant recognition from managers. In fact, the study concluded that the most effective ways to motivate employees are (1) personal thanks from the manager, (2) written thanks from the manager, (3) promotion for performance, (4) public praise, and (5) morale-building meetings. Many have said that these results are just plain common sense.

Common sense, perhaps. But common practice?

Graham matched these findings with employee studies showing that 58 percent seldom (if ever) are thanked by their manager for a job well done, 76 percent seldom (if ever) receive written thanks from their manager, 78 percent seldom (if ever) receive promotions based upon performance, 81 percent seldom (if ever) receive public praise in the workplace, and 92 percent seldom (if ever) participate in morale-building meetings.

So what did Graham conclude? "It appears that the techniques that have the greatest motivational impact are practiced the least, even though they are easier and less expensive to use."

Even with all of this empirical data as support for the importance of higher-level human needs, most managers still refuse to believe it — or, perhaps more accurately, refuse to act upon the evidence.

Which takes more personal energy — to increase a satisfier or increase a motivator? Giving a bonus or a reprimand is infinitely easier than giving specific, constructive praise or arranging morale-building meetings. In short, motivators require us to extend ourselves, to sacrifice and serve in order to meet the deeper-level needs in people. The old employee proverb says, "My pay is my right. Your praise is your gift."

For years, many scoffed and poked fun at how the folks at businesses like Mary Kay would regularly conduct wild and crazy recognitional and morale-building meetings. In the year 2004, those wild and crazy meetings are still being conducted at what is far and away the most successful business on the planet: Wal-Mart.

Nobody seems to be laughing any more.

NO WAY, BABY—SHOW ME THE MONEY!

Yet skeptics still abound.

My audiences will often put up with hearing these stories, but afterward the brave ones will come to me and say, "Come on, Jim, the praise-and-recognition stuff is all fine and nice, but really it's just smoke and mirrors. In the end, all that really matters is the money, Jim. Don't let 'em fool ya." All that really matters to them is "Show me the money, baby!"

Now, please do not get me wrong. Money is important. Just hold payroll for one week, and you will quickly see how important it is. The point is that employee compensation must be *fair,* both internally and externally equitable. This means that you do not need to be paying the most in town, but you probably should not be paying the least. However, once compensation is perceived to be "fair" and the need is "satisfied," its value as a motivator greatly diminishes. Says Jon Katzenbach, coauthor of the bestselling book *The Wisdom of Teams,* "While money may attract and retain people, it is rarely at the heart of what motivates them to excel."

As mentioned earlier, I spent many years as a labor consultant in Detroit. I was involved in more than a hundred union representation campaigns in which my job was to convince the voting employees that the union was not a good idea, even when it sometimes clearly was! There were times I would have voted for the union if I were in their shoes! I would go into some of the most hostile and intimidating environments you can imagine.

When I asked the rank and file what the problem was, what do you think I would hear? You guessed it. Money. The CEO would tell me it was about money, the supervisors would tell me it was about money, and Chucky driving the forklift would tell me it was about money. But guess what? It was *never* about money.

It took me several years to figure it out, but labor problems were *always* about failed relationships. People would point to money because it was something tangible that they could get their arms around.

Things like trust, appreciation, respect, kindness, and caring were just not things these tough guys wanted to talk about. Yet that was always the underlying issue: "We don't trust you anymore. You don't have our best interests at heart. You don't appreciate what we do here. You can now talk to these guys from the union — they'll do our talking for us."

I remember once being confronted by a rather raucous and unruly teamster official who got in my face and challenged me on this point by *insisting* that money was a long-term motivator. To calm things down, I decided to ask him a question: "How much effort do you give at work now?" He proudly proclaimed, "One hundred and ten percent!" Ignoring the fact that it is impossible to give more than 100 percent, I then asked, "How much will you give at work if they double your pay today?" Again he exclaimed, "One hundred and ten percent" before adding, "How come they are both the same?"

Think of marriage, which is an organization of two people joined together for a purpose. In the United States, roughly 50 percent of these organizations fail. Do you know the number one reason given for the failure? Money. Financial difficulty is the number one reason given for the failure of marriages in America. Now, do you believe that? That must mean that people in lower socioeconomic situations have a much higher rate of divorce. Indeed, poor people must be incapable of having happy marriages. Of course, we all know how ridiculous that is. Failed marriages are the result of failed relationships. But it's easier and less painful to just point to the money.

WHAT MOTIVATES VOLUNTEERS?

If you are still convinced that money is the bottom line for motivating people, then answer this question:

How do volunteer organizations get people from the neck up? How do volunteer organizations get people to commit their time, talents, and other resources to their cause for no money whatsoever?

At a church I used to attend, there was a middle-aged man who was, I believed, the most motivated guy I had ever met. Every time I drove by the church, I would see him hanging from the steeple with a paintbrush, hand-cutting acres of lawn, changing lightbulbs, doing landscaping — you name it. The guy was always busting his tail working on that church.

Some time later, I happened to talk to his employer, who gave me another perspective. When I told him how motivated this guy was around the church, his employer was shocked! As his boss put it, "If he was any lazier at work, I think his heart would stop beating."

If money motivated people to work hard, that would mean that the automotive employees where I live (Detroit) would be the hardest-working people in America, right? Without getting specific, I can tell you that is not the case.

Now, what motivated that man at the church to do what he did around the church but not at work?

To begin with, that church had excellent leadership that had influenced him in very positive ways. The leadership had no "power" over him but had developed "authority" (influence) with him. They had served him by identifying and meeting his legitimate needs over the years.

Second, he bought into the mission and purpose of the church and believed he was involved in something special, something important. This purpose and meaning met higher-level needs in him and motivated him to action.

Third, rarely did a month go by in which the leadership did not publicly recognize and appreciate his contributions to the team. The pastor in his sermons often found a way to appreciate his contributions by saying things like "By the way, did you all see the job he did waxing the pews?" At the annual church business meeting, he was regularly awarded a medal or plaque for his generous service. In short, he felt valued, respected, and appreciated for his efforts. People cared about him. He felt *needed*.

Fourth, he was part of a team committed to excellence, and that excited him. The leadership team was committed to training and developing its people to better serve and meet the mission of the organization. There was excellence in everything the church did, from the way it ran its Sunday school, to the way it built homes for the homeless, to the way the pastor prepared his sermons.

Fifth, he felt he was part of a special community where he could share his joys, dreams, sorrows, and concerns without fear of ridicule or condemnation. He had grown to really love the people on *his* team and genuinely enjoyed their company. In short, he felt "safe" there.

OTHER ESSENTIALS

The most successful organizations I have encountered understand and work diligently to meet the deeper needs that human beings all share.

I believe those deeper human needs include:
- A need for great leadership
- A need for meaning and purpose
- A need to be appreciated, recognized, and respected
- A need to be part of something excellent (special)
- A need to be part of a caring community

DEVELOP GREAT LEADERS

I have written two books on leadership, so it is safe to say that I am convinced excellent leadership is essential to meeting human needs and operating a successful organization.

One of the major themes of this book is that leadership is a skill that can be learned, practiced, and developed. Unfortunately, most organizations in America do not treat leadership as a skill even though they may agree that it is a skill. Here is what I mean.

Let's say you start a business in which the main asset consists of a large and highly complex machine that you locate in the middle of the floor in your ten-thousand-square-foot warehouse.

Now, this piece of high-tech equipment is essential to your organization because it controls the quality and quantity of your products. This gizmo is completely automated and can even box, label, and mail your product. The downside of this marvelous piece of technology is that if it breaks down, your business breaks down. In fact, without this contraption you are out of business. Clearly, it is your "greatest asset."

Now it is time for you to decide who you will hire to do the maintenance on this great asset to ensure that it is performing at an optimal level. This new hire will perform the critical preventive maintenance to prevent future breakdowns that could cripple your organization and cause your already-exorbitant business-interruption insurance premiums to skyrocket. Who will you hire?

Will you just post the job and take the most senior person who applies? How about the best forklift driver? Will you hire a flunky brother-in-law to come in and service this asset? How about after sending him to a daylong seminar?

Of course not.

You would hire the very best technician you could find. You would constantly be challenging this person to continually improve his or her skills and keep up with the newest technology. You would not hesitate to pay for the best training and development available to keep his or her skills current. You would probably spare no expense to be sure you had the very best person possible servicing your "greatest asset."

If you make decisions at a high level in your organization and you agree that leadership is identifying and meeting the needs of your people, what is the greatest need your people, your greatest assets, have? They need the best leadership, the best technicians you can get to service these great assets. Great organizations understand this principle. Remember, there are no weak platoons, only weak leaders.

One more point about developing leaders. I learned in HR 101 more than twenty-five years ago that the most important person in ensuring positive employee relations is the frontline supervisor. I heard that statement quoted many times but never really believed it. I always thought it was really the HR person, possibly the general manager, or perhaps even the CEO. After all these years, guess what I now *know?*

The most important person in ensuring positive employee relations is the frontline supervisor. Period.

Yes, the HR guy might have an outgoing personality; the general manager might be a wonderful, principled woman; and the CEO might be a nice-looking person who gives great speeches. But the reality for the people on the front lines is their direct supervisor. If they've got a lousy boss, they've got a lousy job. End of story. They have to live with *that* reality for 50 percent of their waking hours.

If *that* reality does not have everything employees need to be their best, look out. Remember, two-thirds of employees do not quit their company — they quit their boss.

CREATE MEANING AND PURPOSE

Human beings have a deep yearning for meaning and purpose in their lives and will give back to organizations who assist them in meeting that need.

People want to believe that what they are doing is important, that it serves a purpose and adds value to the world. People want to know that their organization stands for something important and is principled in its behavior. People crave something out of the ordinary, something that brings out the best in them. People are yearning for ways to find alignment between their personal values and the values of their organization. People hunger for a way to live out their lives in a meaningful and fulfilling way.

One of the leader's main purposes, then, is to be a "missionary" of sorts, reminding people about what the organization stands for, what it values, what it is trying to accomplish, and who is being served. A missionary to remind people about "the rules of the house" and what conduct and behaviors the team is committed to live by. Someone to remind people about what is special about them and what is special about the work they are doing.

ServiceMaster, the highly successful Fortune 500 company headquartered near Chicago, is a marvelous example of a corporation that provides purpose and meaning to its seventy-five-thousand-plus employees. Many of its employees are engaged in some of the most undesirable and mundane of tasks, from cleaning toilets to killing cockroaches. Yet most ServiceMaster associates could easily tell you why what their company does is important and why what they do is improving the human condition.

If meaning and purpose are not obviously evident in what you do as an organization, *find* the meaning. Your organization is meeting a need in society or it would not exist. Your purpose can simply be meeting that need better than anyone else. At the very least, your organization is providing sustenance for all its employees, spouses, sons, daughters, customers, and vendors, so a lot is at stake if your organization fails. Get excited about that! Develop a passion even if you have to fake it to make it. As Aristotle would probably say, "Act passionately and you will develop passion." Behave with passion and your people will catch it, too.

In summary, it is vital to convincingly articulate how your organization serves human needs and makes the world a better place. It is crucial to build your organization on principles everyone understands and believes in beyond just the short-term goal of increasing shareholder value. I know some may not want to hear this, but it is time to face the truth: The mission of "Increasing Shareholder Value" is not very inspiring to most people.

In *Built to Last,* Jim Collins and Jerry Porras say this about the truly great companies: "Yes, they seek profits, but they're equally guided by a core ideology—core values and a sense of purpose beyond just making money."

HONOR PEOPLE

Think of the awesome responsibility we have as leaders to provide a healthy environment for our employees who spend much of their lives at work.

I have been told many times by employees at excellent companies that the best part of their day is going to work because it is the only place in their lives where they are treated with respect and dignity.

Think about that! Think about some of the dreadful environments people go home to after work every day. What a privilege as leaders to have the opportunity to provide a respectful, caring, and safe reprieve for people from some of the gloom of their everyday lives. Their job may be the only place where they receive respect, courtesy, recognition, and a sense of belonging.

Honor your people by giving sincere and specific praise when it is earned, recognizing their achievements, and rewarding excellence. Honor people by showing them that you are sincerely interested in them as people and not just in what they can do for you or your organization. Honor people by insisting upon excellence in all they do. Honor them by helping them build their character and being the best they can be.

I have learned that employees have a subconscious question the leader needs to answer on a regular basis—if not directly, then by his or her actions. That question is simply "Are you glad I'm here?"

Remember, it is the little things that make a house a home. Model the little common courtesies like saying "Please," "Thank you," "I'm sorry; I was wrong," and "What do you think?" Be the first to speak when you walk by someone in the hallway, and find something positive and encouraging to say to people. Practice these behaviors until they become habit. Observe these disciplines until you do not have to *try* to be a good leader—you have *become* a good leader.

One of the deepest needs a human being possesses is the need to be heard. Really heard. Develop the skill of asking open-ended questions, which are simply questions that cannot be answered with a yes or a no. You know how it is with teenagers when you ask, "Where did you go?" and they counter, "Nowhere," and you follow with "What did you do?" and they grunt, "Nothing." You do not learn much asking questions this way.

Learn to ask open-ended questions that begin with

why, what, where, how, what do you think, tell me about, and so on. Here are some examples:

- What do you like about working here?
- What frustrates you about working here?
- What obstacles are in the way of performing your job to the best of your ability?
- How would you assess the feedback you're getting about how you are doing here?
- Tell me about your family.
- What needs do you have here that are not being met?
- If you could change just one thing about your job, what would it be?
- Over the past year, what accomplishments are you most proud of and why?
- Which aspects of your job performance do you believe you need to improve upon?
- What frustrates you most about your job?
- What goals do you have for the coming twelve months? How would you measure these goals?
- What ideas do you have to help improve your department?
- What ideas do you have to help improve this organization?
- How would you assess the commitment of your coworkers to doing a quality job?
- How would you assess your job satisfaction?
- How would you assess my performance as a leader?

- How specifically could I improve as a leader?
- What would you do differently if you were the leader here?
- How can I better support you?
- How could the organization better support you?
- What questions do you have for me?
- How often do you think we should "check in" with each other?
- Tell me about your life and career before you came to work here.

DEMAND EXCELLENCE

I am convinced that the vast majority of people want to be part of something special. They long to be part of an organization they can be proud of, in which the standards for admission are high, daily expectations are high, and people feel good when they go home at night because they know they have worked hard for a good cause.

What is inspiring about working for an organization in which the only two requirements for employment are the ability to fog a mirror and the absence of a toe tag? What is inspiring about working for an organization whose people perform with mediocrity and do just enough to "get by"?

I find so many managers who are afraid to demand excellence because they fear it will drive people away—at least that is the excuse given. Excellence drives mediocre people away just as mediocrity drives the superstars away.

Leaders must maintain high standards and demand

excellence because excellence builds a healthy pride and confidence. When people begin accomplishing goals and achieving results, their confidence level rises, and they begin to set even larger goals for themselves and their organization. This excellence then becomes contagious, which is an essential ingredient for being the best. When the tide rises in the harbor, all boats must either sink or rise with it.

Major General James Ulio made this point in 1943 when he told a class of newly commissioned officers, "Morale is when a soldier thinks his army is the best in the world; his regiment the best in the army; his company the finest in the regiment; his squad the best in the company; and that he himself is the best damned soldier in the whole outfit."

Effective leaders are never satisfied with the status quo because they are continually striving to be better. They are not too proud to look outside their unit to discover the best practices of others and "borrow" what they can to achieve even greater excellence. They are committed to being the very best, which inspires those around them to also be the best. Not everyone can generate sales like Wal-Mart or profits like Microsoft, but every person and every organization is capable of being the best *they* can be.

Have you ever been part of a truly excellent team? Perhaps it was a winning athletic team, scholastic panel, business entity, military unit, or religious group. Think about the sense of pride, accomplishment, and confidence you had just being associated with success. Think about how motivating it was to go the extra mile for the team. Have you ever had a child on a winning team? Did you have to motivate him or her to go to practice or to games? Excellence becomes its own motivation and ignites the fire within.

This quest for excellence is contagious, and once people in the unit understand that the leader is committed to excellence, people and the organization begin to rise to levels they never dreamed they were capable of.

And they will look around one day at what they have built and exclaim, "How did this all happen?"

BUILD COMMUNITY

I was recently on a flight from Houston to Boston and had the good fortune to meet a retired Marine Corps captain, probably in his mid-fifties.

I have been interested in the marines for some time because of the great reputation the Corps has of building quality, disciplined, and committed individuals who give their all. I thought this would be an excellent person to test some of my ideas of leadership against, so I asked him a simple question.

"Tell me, sir, as an ex-marine, how do the marines get people so committed to being the best?"

Did I get an earful.

His response went something like this.

"Well to begin with, Jim, I am not an ex-marine. There is no such thing as an ex-marine or a former marine, because we are marines for life. We may be reserve marines, retired marines, or marine veterans, but once a marine, always a marine. The commitment never dies.

"As far as being the best and being committed, that part is easy to explain. The Marine Corps is an exclusive club with high standards of which we are proud to be a part. You do not *join* the marines—you *become* a marine. Many wash out, because the Corps has very high standards, and it is no cakewalk becoming a marine.

"When one becomes a marine, he or she is proud of what he or she has become. Being marines means we stand for duty, honor, and commitment, and this provides us with purpose and meaning. And once you commit to standing for those things, you would rather die than not live up to your commitment.

"Finally, I would say the greatest motivator of all is the love and respect we marines have for one another. The last thing you would ever want to do as a marine is let your platoon or your buddy down. Really, Jim, it's not about doing it for the flag or doing it for the sergeant. It's about doing it for these people I respect so much."

Building community is going about the business of creating a healthy environment in which people can live and work free of unnecessary barriers and distractions. Many great organizations possess this capacity to create an environment in which the differences—social, political, ethnic, positional, racial, and others—are transcended. They struggle to create a place where committed yet diverse people can find common ground to work together toward goals identified as being for the common good. Great organizations work to reduce or eliminate unnecessary barriers like politics, positional power, head games, and secret agendas that suck the positive energy right out of people and the organization.

Community is not a place free from conflict. Indeed, when two or more people are gathered together for a purpose, there will be conflict—at least there *should* be in a healthy community. Community is a place not of conflict avoidance but of conflict resolution, where members have learned to stop avoiding their differences and have learned to deal with conflict head-on in respectful ways. Members have learned to behave with respect, to listen, to be assertive with one another, to be open to new challenges, and to value the diversity present in any healthy team.

Building community is creating a place where people feel "safe" to be themselves and are freed up to put all their energy and resources into the things that will make themselves and their organization great. Think of how creative and inspired a group could become if the members could just get most of the unnecessary barriers out of the way. Imagine what an amazing problem-solving body a group working in community could become.

Community is rarely built by accident, although we may see glimmers of it in response to a crisis. Yet when the crisis passes, the old barriers typically snap right back into place and people go right back to the old games. Genuine community is developed by practicing the proper principles that ensure healthy relationships. Principles such as the Golden Rule, assertive communication, building trust, and others discussed earlier.

Mike Krzyzewski, Duke University's men's basketball head coach for the past twenty-four years, has amassed an amazing 601–176 record at Duke, the best college-basketball coaching record over the past two decades.

Asked about his success, he talks about the influence of his wife and three daughters: "Over the years, the girls have exposed me to an environment where they share their feelings, and I've tried to teach my players to do the same thing. I tell them it's not guys doing girl things; it's being a real person—to hug, to cry, to laugh, to share. If you create a culture where that's allowed, all of a sudden you have some depth."

Building community is the dynamic that enables groups like the Dale Carnegie Course, Alcoholics Anonymous, and Weight Watchers to achieve the amazing results they are famous for. They get members to set aside their differences and talk about things that matter.

When groups learn to set aside the barriers that get in the way of healthy relationships and team viability, it is absolutely amazing how these groups grow and become effective teams able to achieve real results.

WHAT ABOUT THESE YOUNG KIDS TODAY?

I often get complaints from baby boomers about their Generation X and Y employees. They complain that "these kids" are not loyal, won't work hard for a living, are self-centered, blah, blah, blah.

Of course, the World War II generation said this about my baby-boom generation, and Socrates' parents said the same about his generation. My experience is that these young people are no better or worse than my generation or the generations before us. Different? Yes. Better or worse, no.

I find these young people have a real "nose" for insincerity, and if you don't pass the "sniff test," they will write you off in a heartbeat. For example, nothing is more repugnant to them than working for some clueless, chain-smoking, command-and-control dictator who delights in looking down the front of the women's blouses when he walks by their desks, who then preaches to them a crock of baloney about company values, integrity, and respect for the individual.

These 50 million Gen Xers and now another 80 million Gen Ys coming up are different indeed. These folks are products of the broken-relationship generation, meaning that if they themselves are not from a broken family, then most of their friends probably are. They have heard all of the cheap talk, promises, and patronizing talk before from insincere and uncommitted adults and former family members. Simply put, if you don't walk your talk, you lose them. As Albert Schweitzer put it, "Example is not the main thing in influencing others. It is the *only* thing."

They tend to be impatient and want it now! They can be disrespectful because they respect accomplishments, not their elders or titles; they are image-driven, as evidenced by tattoos and body piercing; they are expressive and will speak their minds openly without holding back. Most of all, they are skeptical of institutions, having grown up in an era in which shame and disgrace have rocked American institutions, from politics to business and from the church to the military.

On the other hand, they are self-reliant, adaptable, innovative, electronic- and computer-literate, technologically oriented, efficient multitaskers, resilient, and tolerant and supportive of diversity. Best of all, they can be very committed and intensely loyal, even fanatical, to people or institutions who meet their higher-level needs for meaning and purpose, to those leaders who "walk their talk," and to those leaders who are the real thing.

Yes, they may well be content to put in their forty hours and fully live their lives, but rather than judge or complain about it, perhaps we should just accept it for what it is. If their forty-hour workweek is on one side of the pendulum extreme, their seventy-hour workweek parents are on the other extreme.

Maybe we can learn something from each other.

IN CLOSING

I want to close by sharing with you a few of the most important lessons I have gleaned from the most successful organizations I have had the privilege of serving over the years.

- Never forget that to lead is to serve.
- Be *very* picky about the people you hire.
- Celebrate a new hire's "acceptance" to your team and orient him or her properly. Never underestimate the power of first impressions.
- Define the purpose and meaning of the work you

are doing, and be passionate about preaching
it over and over and over again.

- Find ways to make people's work more
  challenging, interesting, and rewarding.
- Compensate people fairly.
- Give honor to all people.
- Identify, develop, and invest heavily in
  your leaders.
- Demand excellence and accountability,
  especially in your leaders.
- Insist upon personal continuous
  improvement.
- Recognize and reward achievements spontaneously.
- Build community.
- Seek out best practices and implement them.
- Push decision-making to the lowest level possible.
- Train your people well and help them develop
  new skills.
- Trust your people to do the right thing.
- Be honest and demand honesty, even brutal
  honesty, including the good news and the bad
  (guess what, they can take it — they have
  had worse news before).
- Respect the important balance between work
  and home life.
- Do the little things that make a house a home.

On a Personal Note

Love cures people —
both the ones who give it
and the ones who receive it.

DR. KARL MENNINGER

AS I REFLECT UPON HUMAN NATURE AND CHANGE, I AM left with the nagging notion that there is something more than just "willpower" and "habit breaking" involved when human beings become resolved to change and grow.

To be sure, change and growth require cooperative "patients" who must do their part, which has been a major theme of this book. But more than that, I have observed that when people begin practicing the behaviors of love, extending themselves for others, they change. And they often change in ways beyond what they expected or thought possible. Simply put, I have come to believe that love changes people.

Of course, this thought is not new—great thinkers, writers, philosophers, theologians, and poets have extolled the virtues of love for several thousand years.

My chosen faith teaches that the Bible is the inspired word of God. In the New Testament, an astonishing claim is made about God and about love. It states, "The one who does not love does not know God, for God is love" (1 John 4:8). Please note that the last three words in this passage do not say that "God acts with love" or that "God is like love." Rather, God *is* love. *Literally*.

I certainly cannot explain the theology or metaphysics behind this well-known passage. Those things are probably best left to the theologians and scholars, anyway. But the longer I ponder the principles of love and the character of God revealed in the Bible, the more I believe I am beginning to understand what John was saying so long ago.

Recently it struck me that if love changes people, which I *know* it does, it would seem to follow that God is the source of the change and growth, because He *is* love. Put another way, when people begin loving others through their efforts and behavior, God has the opportunity to work in the lives of both the giver and the receiver.

Oswald Chambers, one of the most insightful Christian thinkers of the past one hundred years, authored a profound little devotional entitled *My Utmost for His Highest,* which is read daily by millions around the world, including our current president. For the May 10 reading, Chambers counsels us to remember that "we cannot do what God does, and that God will not do what we can do. We cannot save ourselves nor sanctify ourselves, God does that; but God will not give us good habits, He will not give us character, He will not make us walk aright. We have to do all that ourselves, we have to work out the salvation God has worked in."

My prayer for this book is that it may awaken some to action. If *you* feel that stirring, please do not wait another day before taking your first steps on the most exciting, difficult, and rewarding journey this side of heaven.

JIM HUNTER
February 2004

APPENDIX 1: LEADERSHIP SKILLS INVENTORY

Manager Name _____

Position _____ Department _____

Please check (✓) appropriate box — If you have no opinion
about a particular statement, please leave the boxes blank

	STRONGLY AGREE	AGREE	DISAGREE	STRONGLY DISAGREE
1. Gives appreciation to others	❏	❏	❏	❏
2. Confronts people with problems/situations as they arise	❏	❏	❏	❏
3. Spends time walking floor and stays close to subordinate activity	❏	❏	❏	❏
4. Gives encouragement to others	❏	❏	❏	❏
5. Makes clear to subordinates what is expected on the job	❏	❏	❏	❏
6. Is a good listener	❏	❏	❏	❏
7. Coaches/counsels employees to ensure compliance with goals	❏	❏	❏	❏
8. Treats people with respect (i.e., like they are important people)	❏	❏	❏	❏
9. Is actively involved in the development of subordinates	❏	❏	❏	❏
10. Holds people accountable for meeting the standards set	❏	❏	❏	❏
11. Gives credit to those who deserve it	❏	❏	❏	❏
12. Shows patience and self-control with others	❏	❏	❏	❏
13. Is a leader people feel confident following	❏	❏	❏	❏
14. Has the technical skills necessary to do the job	❏	❏	❏	❏
15. Meets the legitimate needs (as opposed to wants) of others	❏	❏	❏	❏
16. Is able to forgive mistakes and not hold grudges	❏	❏	❏	❏
17. Is someone people can trust	❏	❏	❏	❏
18. Does not engage in backstabbing others (talking behind backs, etc.)	❏	❏	❏	❏
19. Gives positive feedback to subordinates when appropriate	❏	❏	❏	❏
20. Does not embarrass people or punish them in front of others	❏	❏	❏	❏
21. Sets high goals for self, subordinates, and department	❏	❏	❏	❏
22. Has a positive attitude on the job	❏	❏	❏	❏
23. Is sensitive to the implications of their decisions on other depts.	❏	❏	❏	❏
24. Is a fair and consistent leader and leads by example	❏	❏	❏	❏
25. Is not an over-controlling or over-domineering person	❏	❏	❏	❏

What are the greatest leadership strengths/skills that the person being evaluated possesses?

_____

_____

What leadership skills does the person being evaluated need to work on and improve?

_____

_____

Your Name _____

Position _____   Department _____

	STRONGLY AGREE	AGREE	DISAGREE	STRONGLY DISAGREE
1. I give appreciation to others	❏	❏	❏	❏
2. I confront people with problems/situations as they arise	❏	❏	❏	❏
3. I spend time walking floor and staying close to subordinate activity	❏	❏	❏	❏
4. I give encouragement to others	❏	❏	❏	❏
5. I make clear to subordinates what is expected on the job	❏	❏	❏	❏
6. I am a good listener	❏	❏	❏	❏
7. I coach and counsel subordinates to ensure compliance with goals	❏	❏	❏	❏
8. I treat people with respect (i.e., like they are important people)	❏	❏	❏	❏
9. I am actively involved in the development of subordinates	❏	❏	❏	❏
10. I hold people accountable for meeting the standards set	❏	❏	❏	❏
11. I give credit to those who deserve it	❏	❏	❏	❏
12. I show patience and self-control with others	❏	❏	❏	❏
13. I am a leader people feel confident following	❏	❏	❏	❏
14. I have the technical skills necessary to do my job	❏	❏	❏	❏
15. I meet the legitimate needs (as opposed to wants) of others	❏	❏	❏	❏
16. I am able to forgive mistakes and not hold grudges	❏	❏	❏	❏
17. I am someone people can trust	❏	❏	❏	❏
18. I do not engage in backstabbing others (talking behind backs, etc.)	❏	❏	❏	❏
19. I give positive feedback to subordinates when appropriate	❏	❏	❏	❏
20. I do not embarrass people or punish them in front of others	❏	❏	❏	❏
21. I set high goals for myself, my subordinates, and my department	❏	❏	❏	❏
22. I have a positive attitude on the job	❏	❏	❏	❏
23. I am sensitive to the implications of my decisions on other depts.	❏	❏	❏	❏
24. I am a fair and consistent leader and lead by example	❏	❏	❏	❏
25. I am not an over-controlling or over-domineering person	❏	❏	❏	❏

What are my greatest Leadership strengths/skills?

_____

_____

What Leadership skills do I need to work on and improve?

_____

Your Signature _____   Date _____

APPENDIX 3: LEADERSHIP SKILLS INVENTORY SUMMARY

NAME: William Johnson   POSITION: Operations Manager
OF SURVEYS RETURNED: 11

	Self Score 3.8	Composite Score 3.0	EVALUATIONS BY SUBORDINATES, PEERS, AND SUPERVISORS: NUMBER OF RESPONDENTS WHO:			
			STRONGLY AGREE	AGREE	DISAGREE	STRONGLY DISAGREE
Has the technical skills necessary for job	4	3.6	7	1	1	0
Is someone people can trust	4	3.6	5	4	0	0
Is not an over-controlling or over-domineering person	4	3.6	5	4	0	0
Gives encouragement to other	4	3.4	4	5	0	0
Treats others with respect	4	3.4	4	5	0	0
Gives positive feedback when appropriate	4	3.4	4	5	0	0
Does not embarrass/punish in front of others	4	3.4	4	5	0	0
Gives appreciation to others	4	3.3	3	6	0	0
Makes clear to subordinates what is expected on the job	4	3.3	3	6	0	0
Gives credit to those who deserve it	4	3.3	3	6	0	0
Does not engage in backstabbing others	4	3.2	4	4	1	0
Is a good listener	4	3.0	3	4	0	1
Is a leader people feel confident following	3	3.0	2	6	1	0
Displays a positive attitude on the job	4	2.9	3	4	2	0
Shows patience and self-control with others	4	2.8	4	2	3	0
Is able to forgive mistakes and not hold grudges	4	2.8	2	4	2	0
Confronts people with problems/situations as they arise	3	2.6	2	4	3	0
Holds people accountable for meeting standards of job	3	2.2	1	4	4	0
Is a fair, consistent, and predictable leader	4	2.2	1	4	4	0
Meets the legitimate needs (as opposed to wants) of others	3	1.8	1	3	3	2

SCORING 0.0 – 2.3   URGENT PROBLEM AREA
2.4 – 2.7   POTENTIAL PROBLEM AREA
2.8 – 3.1   GOOD SHAPE
3.2 – 4.0   EXCELLENT SHAPE

NAME: **William Johnson**

WHAT ARE THE GREATEST LEADERSHIP STRENGTHS/ SKILLS THAT THE PERSON BEING EVALUATED POSSESSES?

"I am very supportive toward the people I supervise or work with. I am a very positive person. My greatest need is seeing my people succeeding on the job and I will do anything to make this happen."

- Keeps open communication with all employees. Is always accessible. Responds quickly to requests for assistance. Is fair, but firm in decision-making.
- Positive attitudes toward others. Willing to take other duties when one of the staff asks him to.
- Desire to succeed.
- Positive attitude, good technical skills, analytical, loves relay, good sense of humor.
- Fair and consistent, clearly supports his team, listens to recommendations and individual situations before making a decision.
- I think he has a great ability to work with someone if they have a problem. He is very patient in showing someone how to do something.
- Bill is excellent with both his peers and subordinates. He is a motivator. He enhances departmental morale with his pleasing personality.
- People person, people enjoy working for him.

WHAT LEADERSHIP SKILLS DOES THE PERSON BEING EVALUATED NEED TO WORK ON AND IMPROVE?

"I need to control my emotions when I get upset during meetings. I need to work on gaining trust from my superiors by continuing to find ways to impress and win their respect."

- Keep subordinates informed of his own schedule or changes, maintain more caution when discussing employee issues.
- Achieve in asking others what he needs to do besides sitting and watching over the floor (if need to do some work).
- Holding people accountable.
- Needs to be unbiased and fair, treat everyone the same, not favoritism with buddies.
- Most of the OM's do not have any training in call processing therefore cannot adequately make decisions when assisting on call-processing issues. Does not hold others accountable for inferior work performance. Tries to play the nice guy all the time, tends to vent in small circus and project negative feelings.
- I think that sometimes he shows a little favoritism to some of his people in not disciplining them for something that they have done and someone has brought it to his attention.
- Consistency, patience, ensuring his team members have the knowledge to properly do their jobs. Not do it for them. Draw a thicker line with subordinates as mgr. to subordinate vs. mgr. to friend.
- Accountability, does not hold his employees accountable for deadlines.

APPENDIX 4: SMART ACTION PLAN*

Name _____ **Position** _____ **Date** _____

SPECIFIC: State your goal/objective *and* how you will accomplish this goal in very specific terms. (Example: *I will give more sincere appreciation to my direct reports. I will give sincere and specific appreciation to at least two (2) people per day.*)

State goal/objective and how you will accomplish it:

_____

_____

MEASURABLE: State how improvement/progress will be tracked and measured. (Example: *I will keep a log in my Palm Pilot of the name of the person and the content of the appreciation given.*)

State how objective will be measured:

_____

_____

ACHIEVABLE: State how this is a realistic and achievable goal, yet also provides a "stretch" for you. (Example: *Giving people appreciation has never been easy for me but twice per day should be "doable."*)

Discuss the "stretch" and "achievability" of this goal:

_____

_____

RELEVANT: State why your objective is relevant and appropriate toward meeting company objectives. (Example: *Receiving sincere appreciation is a legitimate human need, and my role as leader is to meet legitimate needs. This is a weak area for me and one I need to improve upon.*)

State why your objective is relevant and appropriate:

_____

_____

TIME-BOUND: State time objectives that will be met. (Example: *I will measure progress daily over the next ninety (90) day period: October 1 – December 31, 2003.*)

State the time frame for actions and measurables:

_____

_____

*One (1) SMART Action Plan per objective. Attach additional sheets if necessary.

Acknowledgments

To my clients, who have taught me many of the valuable lessons contained herein.

To the folks at First Baptist Church, who provide a community of love and support for me and my family.

To my parents, Jack and Phyllis Hunter, for their example, love, and support throughout the years.

To Rachael (my favorite daughter), for the person she is and the richness she brings to my life.

And finally, to Denise, my life partner, best friend, and wife. Without her, little, if any, of this would be possible.